a
cook's
book
of
sauces

mayonnaise
hollandaise
béarnaise

Published by Murdoch Books Pty Limited.
www.murdochbooks.com.au

Murdoch Books Australia
Pier 8/9, 23 Hickson Road
Millers Point NSW 2000
Phone: + 61 (0) 2 8220 2000
Fax: + 61 (0) 2 8220 2558

Murdoch Books UK Limited
Erico House, 6th Floor
93–99 Upper Richmond Road
Putney, London SW15 2TG
Phone: + 44 (0) 20 8785 5995
Fax: + 44 (0) 20 8785 5985

Chief Executive: Juliet Rogers
Publisher: Kay Scarlett

Design and Illustration: Alex Frampton
Cover Design: Marylouise Brammer
Photographer: Natasha Milne
Stylist: Sarah O'Brien
Project Manager: Zoë Harpham
Editor: Justine Harding
Introduction text: Leanne Kitchen
Recipes developed by the Murdoch Books Test Kitchen
Production: Kita George

National Library of Australia Cataloguing-in-Publication Data
Mayonnaise, hollandaise, béarnaise. Includes index. ISBN 9781741963946.
1. Cookery (Mayonnaise). 2. Sauces. 641.814

Printed by Midas Printing (Asia) Ltd in 2005. PRINTED IN CHINA.
Reprinted 2008.

IMPORTANT: Those who might be at risk from the effects of salmonella poisoning
(the elderly, pregnant women, young children and those suffering from immune
deficiency diseases) should consult their doctor with any concerns about eating raw eggs.

OVEN GUIDE: You may find cooking times vary depending on the oven you are using.
For fan-forced ovens, as a general rule, set the oven temperature to 20°C (35°F)
lower than indicated in the recipe.

a cook's book of sauces

mayonnaise hollandaise béarnaise

MURDOCH BOOKS

Contents

the magic of sauce

Imagine a world without sauce. There'd be no gravy for roasts, no pesto for pasta and, minus the vinegary kick of a salad dressing, lettuce would be a bland proposition indeed. Take away the zing of salsa, the tang of garlic-rich aïoli and the piquant hit of an unctuous horseradish cream, and dining is dull. Sauces add finesse. They finish a dish, offering up flavours and textures that complement what's already on the plate. They elevate good, easy food (a perfectly chargrilled steak, a simple, leafy salad, a wedge of warming pudding, for instance) into a memorable meal. Whether an uncomplicated affair (a pile of berries reduced to a suave purée at the flick of a processor switch perhaps, or an undemanding melt of chocolate, cream and butter) or a somewhat more ambitious, simmered-for-hours concoction, the rewards of sauce-making are great. Quite simply, with sauce, the dining table is a far more interesting place to be.

Sauces are universal, traversing cultures and climates; they come to us from the four corners of the globe. We've the French to thank for sophisticated emulsions (think of opulent hollandaise or the cool, velvet touch of mayonnaise), useful roux (impossible to make classic macaroni cheese or lobster mornay without one of these) and the lush cream- and butter-based substances that spoon perfectly over fish or chicken. Greece offers up skordalia, a tantalizing amalgam of garlic, mashed potato and aromatic olive oil while Mexico has given the world rustic, punchy salsas. Pungent flavours (chilli, soy and fish sauces, exotic spices and herbs) spike myriad combinations from South East Asia, and what would one possibly serve with roast turkey had the New World not shared its cranberry sauce?

Sauce-making has suffered the reputation of being a tricky culinary discipline to master, but really, this is undeserved. Very little is needed in the way of special equipment, and modern kitchen devices (food processors, blenders and electric beaters) have minimized the slog involved in puréeing, sieving and emulsifying by hand. Required skills run to basic whisking, stirring and skimming and, occasionally, the exertion of a little patience. The rewards of expanding one's sauce repertoire are great; sauces, fundamentally, are quite delicious things. 'A well-made sauce will make even an elephant or a grandfather palatable,' quipped one nineteenth century wag; and while this theory doesn't beg testing, it is true that a sauce, whether it is smooth and silky or thick and chunky, will elevate even everyday dishes to memorable, impressive feasts.

Aioli Salsa Verde Vinaigrette Gravy Espag

Savoury

le Pesto Mayonnaise Hollandaise Béarnaise

Aïoli (Garlic Mayonnaise)

Serves 6

6 garlic cloves
2 egg yolks
250 ml (9 fl oz/1 cup) olive oil
lemon juice, optional

1. Blend the garlic cloves, egg yolks and a pinch of salt in a blender until a thick paste forms.

2. With the motor running, add the olive oil, drop by drop, until the aïoli is thick and creamy. If it becomes too thick, add a little lemon juice. Season to taste. This recipe can also be made using a mortar and pestle.

 Serve with salads, egg dishes, fish soup or cold poached fish. Also good with vegetables.

Almond and Red Capsicum Sauce

Serves 6

1 large red capsicum (pepper), seeded and quartered
2 garlic cloves, unpeeled
125 g (4$\frac{1}{2}$ oz/1$\frac{1}{3}$ cups) flaked almonds
80 ml (2$\frac{1}{2}$ fl oz/$\frac{1}{3}$ cup) red wine vinegar
170 ml (5$\frac{1}{2}$ fl oz/$\frac{2}{3}$ cup) olive oil
60 ml (2 fl oz/$\frac{1}{4}$ cup) boiling water
2 tablespoons finely chopped parsley

1 Cook the capsicum, skin side up, under a hot grill (broiler) for 10 minutes. Add the garlic and cook until the capsicum skin blackens and blisters. Cool the garlic and capsicum in a plastic bag, then peel away the skin.

2 Spread the almonds on a baking tray and roast under a moderate grill, stirring once or twice, until lightly golden. Set aside to cool for 5 minutes.

3 Process the peeled capsicum, garlic and almonds in a food processor until smooth. With the motor running, slowly add the vinegar. Season with salt and pepper. Gradually add the oil, then the boiling water. The sauce should have the consistency of mayonnaise. Add the parsley and process briefly. Refrigerate the sauce overnight before serving.

  Serve with lamb cutlets or steaks.

Angel Sauce

Serves 4

125 g (4$^{1}/_{2}$ oz) butter
3 egg yolks
1$^{1}/_{2}$ tablespoons lemon juice
freshly ground white pepper
2 egg whites

1 Gently heat the butter in a saucepan until it begins to bubble. Blend the egg yolks, lemon juice and white pepper in a blender for 5 seconds. With the motor running, slowly add the hot butter in a steady stream. Transfer the sauce to a large bowl and set aside to cool, stirring occasionally to prevent a skin forming on the surface.

2 Beat the egg whites in a small bowl with electric beaters until soft peaks form. Fold the egg whites into the sauce. Refrigerate for at least 30 minutes before serving. (The sauce can be refrigerated for up to 24 hours.)

 Serve over steamed artichokes, green beans or asparagus. Also good with grilled (broiled) fish, smoked salmon, prawns (shrimp), oysters on the half shell or chargrilled scallops.

Apple Sauce

serves 6–8

4 green apples, peeled, cored and chopped
2 teaspoons caster (superfine) sugar
2 cloves
1 cinnamon stick
1–2 teaspoons lemon juice

1 Put the apple, sugar, cloves, cinnamon stick and 125 ml (4 fl oz/1/2 cup) of water in a small saucepan. Cover and simmer over low heat for 10 minutes, or until the apple is soft. Discard the cloves and cinnamon stick.

2 Mash the apple, or press it through a sieve if you want a fine sauce. Stir in the lemon juice, to taste. Serve warm or cold.

 Serve with roast pork, pork chops or pan-fried pork fillet.

Avocado and Chilli Salsa

Serves 4

1¹/₂ teaspoons ground cumin
1 large avocado, finely chopped
1 red onion, very finely chopped
1 small red chilli, seeded and finely chopped
2 teaspoons lemon juice
2 teaspoons olive oil

1 Put the cumin in a dry frying pan and fry, shaking the pan, for about 40 seconds.

2 Combine the cumin, avocado, onion, chilli, lemon juice and olive oil in a bowl.

 Serve with corn chips, pitta bread, chargrilled meats or fish.

Avocado Dressing

Serves 4

1/2 large avocado
1 tablespoon plain yoghurt
1 tablespoon oil
1 teaspoon tarragon vinegar
1 garlic clove, crushed

1 Blend the avocado, yoghurt, oil, tarragon vinegar, garlic
  and 2 tablespoons of water in a blender or food processor
  for 30 seconds, or until the dressing is smooth.

2 Cover the surface of the dressing with plastic wrap and
  refrigerate until ready to serve.

 Serve as a dressing for pasta salad.

Balsamic Vinaigrette

Serves 6

2 tablespoons balsamic vinegar
1 teaspoon dijon mustard
80 ml (2^1/$_2$ fl oz/^{1}/$_3$ cup) extra virgin olive oil
1 small garlic clove

1 Whisk the vinegar and mustard in a small bowl until combined. Gradually beat in the olive oil. Season with salt and freshly ground black pepper.

2 Cut the garlic clove in half, skewer onto a toothpick and leave in the dressing to infuse for at least 1 hour.

  Serve drizzled over a green salad or sliced tomatoes.

Barbecue Sauce

Serves 4

2 teaspoons oil
1 small onion, finely chopped
1 tablespoon malt vinegar
1 tablespoon soft brown sugar
80 ml (2$^1/_2$ fl oz/$^1/_3$ cup) tomato sauce (ketchup)
1 tablespoon worcestershire sauce

1 Heat the oil in a small saucepan over low heat. Cook the onion, stirring occasionally, for 3 minutes, or until soft.

2 Add the vinegar, sugar, tomato sauce and worcestershire sauce and bring to the boil. Reduce the heat and simmer, stirring occasionally, for 3 minutes. Serve warm or at room temperature.

 Serve with hamburgers, barbecued chops, steaks or sausages.

Basil Garlic Dressing

serves 8

1 garlic clove
2 tablespoons chopped basil
60 ml (2 fl oz/¼ cup) lemon juice
125 ml (4 fl oz/½ cup) extra virgin olive oil

1 Process the garlic and basil in a food processor or blender until finely chopped.

2 Add the lemon juice and process in short bursts until the mixture is combined. Gradually add the olive oil and process until combined. Season to taste with salt and freshly ground black pepper.

 Serve with a green salad.

Béarnaise Sauce

Serves 4

80 ml (2¹/₂ fl oz/¹/₃ cup) white wine vinegar
2 spring onions (scallions), roughly chopped
2 teaspoons chopped tarragon
2 egg yolks
125 g (4¹/₂ oz) butter, cubed

1 Put the vinegar, spring onion and tarragon in a small saucepan. Bring to the boil, then reduce the heat slightly and simmer until the mixture has reduced by a third. Set aside to cool completely.

2 Strain the vinegar into a heatproof bowl and add the egg yolks. Place the bowl over a saucepan of barely simmering water and whisk until the mixture is thick and pale.

3 Add the butter, one cube at a time, and whisk after each addition until the mixture is thick and smooth. Season to taste and serve immediately.

 Serve with roast beef or lamb, pan-fried steaks or poached salmon.

Béchamel (White Sauce)

Serves 4

250 ml (9 fl oz/1 cup) milk
1 slice of onion
1 bay leaf
6 peppercorns
30 g (1 oz) butter
1 tablespoon plain (all-purpose) flour
freshly ground white pepper

1 Put the milk, onion, bay leaf and peppercorns in a small saucepan. Bring to the boil, then remove from the heat. Set aside to infuse for 10 minutes, then strain the milk.

2 Melt the butter in a small saucepan and add the flour. Cook, stirring, for 1 minute, or until the mixture is golden and bubbling. Remove from the heat and gradually add the milk, stirring after each addition until completely smooth.

3 Return to the heat and stir until the mixture boils. Continue cooking for 1 minute, or until thick. Season with salt and white pepper. Serve hot.

 Serve with fish, corned beef, steamed cauliflower or steamed broccoli.

Beurre Blanc

Serves 4

2 French shallots, chopped
60 ml (2 fl oz/¼ cup) white wine vinegar
220 g (7¾ oz) unsalted butter, cubed
lemon juice, to taste

1 Put the shallots, vinegar and 60 ml (2 fl oz/¼ cup) of water in a saucepan. Bring to the boil, then reduce the heat and simmer until the mixture is reduced to 2 tablespoons. Strain into a clean saucepan and return to low heat.

2 Whisk in the butter, a few pieces at a time. The sauce will thicken as the butter is added until it is the consistency of cream. Season to taste with salt, pepper and lemon juice and serve warm.

Note: If the sauce is too hot, the butter will separate; too cold and it will set. Keep it warm in a bowl over a saucepan of gently simmering water.

 Serve with seafood, steamed artichoke hearts or steamed or boiled vegetables.

Black Bean Sauce

Serves 6

2 tablespoons salted black beans
1 tablespoon vegetable oil
1 small onion, finely chopped
1 garlic clove, finely chopped
1 tablespoon finely chopped fresh ginger
1 red chilli, seeded and finely chopped
310 ml (10¾ fl oz/1¼ cups) chicken stock
2 teaspoons cornflour (cornstarch)
2 teaspoons sesame oil

1 Rinse the black beans under cold water for 3–4 minutes to remove any excess salt. Drain well.

2 Heat the vegetable oil in a small saucepan over low heat. Add the onion, garlic, ginger and chilli and cook until the onion is soft but not browned. Add the stock and bring to the boil. Reduce the heat and simmer for 5 minutes.

3 Mix the cornflour with 1 tablespoon of water. Add to the sauce and cook, stirring, until the sauce has thickened. Simmer for 3 minutes, then add the black beans and sesame oil and mix well. Serve hot.

 Serve with stir-fried meat or chicken, prawns (shrimp) or crab.

Black Sesame Dressing

Serves 4-6

50 g (1³/4 oz/¹/3 cup) black sesame seeds
1¹/2 teaspoons caster (superfine) sugar
1 tablespoon sake
1¹/2 tablespoons dashi (see note)
2 teaspoons tamari

1 Put the sesame seeds in a dry frying pan and fry over medium heat, stirring regularly, for about 5 minutes, or until aromatic. Immediately transfer the sesame seeds to a mortar.

2 Grind the sesame seeds until very finely crushed. Gradually incorporate the sugar, sake, dashi and tamari until the mixture forms a smooth paste.

Note: To make the dashi, dissolve ¹/4 teaspoon of instant dashi granules in 125 ml (4 fl oz/¹/2 cup) of boiling water and stir until dissolved.

 Serve with blanched or steamed English spinach.

Blackcurrant Sauce

Serves 6

500 ml (17 fl oz/2 cups) red wine
55 g (2 oz/¼ cup) sugar
200 g (7 oz/1²/₃ cups) blackcurrants
1 tablespoon red wine vinegar

1　Put the red wine in a saucepan and bring to the boil. Add the sugar and cook until the mixture has reduced by half.

2　Add the blackcurrants and vinegar and simmer until the blackcurrants are tender. Serve hot.

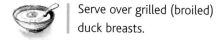 Serve over grilled (broiled) duck breasts.

Blue Cheese Dressing

Serves 6–8

125 g (4¹/2 oz/¹/2 cup) whole-egg mayonnaise
60 ml (2 fl oz/¹/4 cup) thick (double/heavy) cream
1 teaspoon white wine vinegar
1 tablespoon finely snipped chives
50 g (1³/4 oz) blue cheese
freshly ground white pepper

1 Combine the mayonnaise, cream, vinegar and chives in a small bowl.

2 Crumble the blue cheese into the mayonnaise mixture and gently stir to combine. Season to taste with salt and freshly ground white pepper.

 Serve over asparagus, boiled new potatoes or jacket potatoes, or with a green salad.

Blueberry and Mint Vinegar

Makes 750 ml (26 fl oz)

500 ml (17 fl oz/2 cups) white wine vinegar
310 g (11 oz/2 cups) blueberries
8 mint sprigs

1 Put the vinegar, blueberries and half the mint sprigs in a saucepan. Bring to the boil, then reduce the heat and simmer for 5 minutes. Remove from the heat.

2 Discard the mint sprigs and pour the mixture into a warm sterilized jar. Add the remaining mint sprigs, seal and store in a cold place for a week.

3 Line a funnel with muslin and strain the vinegar into warm sterilized bottles. Seal and label. Store for up to a year.

 Use in place of white wine vinegar for a flavoured vinaigrette.

Bread Sauce

Serves 4

2 cloves
1 onion
250 ml (9 fl oz/1 cup) milk
1 bay leaf
55 g (2 oz/²/₃ cup) fresh breadcrumbs
60 ml (2 fl oz/¹/₄ cup) cream (whipping)

1 Push the cloves into the onion and put in a saucepan with the milk and bay leaf. Bring to the boil, then remove from the heat, cover and set aside for 10 minutes. Discard the onion and bay leaf.

2 Add the breadcrumbs to the milk and season. Return to the heat, cover and simmer gently, stirring occasionally, for 10 minutes. Stir in the cream. Serve warm.

 Serve with roast chicken, turkey, goose or game.

Caesar Dressing

Serves 6

1 egg
2 teaspoons white wine vinegar
3 teaspoons dijon mustard
1 anchovy fillet
1 garlic clove, crushed
80 ml (2^1/$_2$ fl oz/^{1}/$_3$ cup) oil

1 Lower the egg into a saucepan of boiling water. Cook for
   1 minute, then drain.

2 Break the egg into a small bowl. Add the vinegar, mustard,
   anchovy and garlic and whisk to combine.

3 Add the oil in a thin stream, whisking continuously, until
   the mixture is smooth and creamy.

 Serve on Caesar salad or any
other green salad.

Calvados Gravy

Serves 8

pan juices from roast pork
1 tablespoon Calvados
2 tablespoons plain (all-purpose) flour
375 ml (13 fl oz/1½ cups) chicken stock
125 ml (4 fl oz/½ cup) unsweetened apple juice

1 Drain off all but 2 tablespoons of the pan juices from the roasting tin. Place the tin on the stove over medium heat. Stir in the Calvados and cook for 1 minute.

2 Remove from the heat, stir in the flour and mix well. Return to the heat and cook, stirring, for 2 minutes. Gradually add the stock and apple juice and cook, stirring, until the gravy has thickened. Season to taste. Serve hot.

 Serve with roast pork.

Caper Sauce

Serves 4

30 g (1 oz) butter
30 g (1 oz/$1/4$ cup) plain (all-purpose) flour
150 ml (5 fl oz) lukewarm milk
150 ml (5 fl oz) lukewarm beef stock
1 tablespoon capers, rinsed and squeezed dry
1–2 teaspoons lemon juice
freshly ground white pepper

1 Melt the butter in a small saucepan, then blend in the flour. Cook, whisking continuously, for 1 minute.

2 Remove from the heat and gradually whisk in the milk and stock. Return to the heat and slowly bring to the boil, whisking until the mixture boils and thickens. Reduce the heat and simmer very gently for 2–3 minutes.

3 Add the capers and lemon juice, to taste. Season with salt and white pepper. Serve hot.

 Serve with veal schnitzel.

Caramelized Onion Sauce

Serves 4-6

40 g (1½ oz) butter
3 onions, sliced
1 tablespoon plain (all-purpose) flour
375 ml (13 fl oz/1½ cups) beef stock
1 tablespoon red wine vinegar

1 Melt the butter in a large saucepan over low heat. Cook the onion for 30 minutes, or until soft and brown. Add the flour and cook, stirring constantly, for 1 minute.

2 Gradually add the stock, stirring constantly until combined. Stir in the vinegar and bring to the boil. Reduce the heat and simmer for 2 minutes. Serve hot or warm.

 Serve with steaks or sausages or on hamburgers.

Champagne Apple Sauce

Serves 6–8

185 ml (6 fl oz/³/4 cup) Champagne or sparkling white wine
4 green apples, peeled, cored and chopped
¹/2 teaspoon finely grated lemon zest
1 tablespoon finely chopped lemon thyme or thyme
40 g (1¹/2 oz) butter, cubed

1   Pour the wine into a saucepan and boil for 1 minute.
Add the apple and lemon zest, cover and simmer for
10 minutes, or until the apple is tender. Stir in the lemon
thyme and set aside to cool for 5 minutes.

2   Purée the apple mixture in a food processor. Gradually add
the butter, processing after each addition. Season to taste
with salt and pepper. Serve warm or at room temperature.

 Serve with roast pork, pan-fried
pork chops, a whole roast ham
or turkey.

Chantilly Hollandaise

Serves 4

175 g (6 oz) butter
125 ml (4 fl oz/¹/₂ cup) cream (whipping)
4 egg yolks
1 tablespoon lemon juice

1 Melt the butter in a small saucepan. Skim any froth from the surface. Set the butter aside to cool.

2 Whip the cream until soft peaks form.

3 Mix the egg yolks with 2 tablespoons of water in a small saucepan. Beat with a wire whisk for 30 seconds, or until the mixture is pale and foamy. Whisk over very low heat for 2–3 minutes, or until the mixture is thick and the whisk leaves a trail — do not let the pan get too hot or the egg yolks will scramble. Remove from the heat.

4 Add the cooled butter, a little at a time, whisking well after each addition. Try to avoid using the milky butter whey in the bottom of the pan. Stir in the lemon juice.

5 Using a metal spoon, fold in the whipped cream. Season to taste and serve immediately.

 Serve with poached or steamed chicken or fish.

Chargrilled Vegetable Salsa

Serves 4

2 roma (plum) tomatoes, halved lengthways

1 small red capsicum (pepper), seeded and halved lengthways

1 small green capsicum (pepper), seeded and halved lengthways

2 small zucchini (courgettes), halved lengthways

2 long thin eggplants (aubergines), halved lengthways

60 ml (2 fl oz/$\frac{1}{4}$ cup) olive oil

2 teaspoons chopped oregano

2 tablespoons chopped flat-leaf (Italian) parsley

1 tablespoon chopped marjoram

2 tablespoons balsamic vinegar

1 Place the vegetables in a large shallow dish. Combine the oil with the oregano, half the parsley and half the marjoram. Pour over the vegetables, toss well and set aside to marinate for at least 2 hours.

2 Heat a barbecue or chargrill pan and cook the vegetables until soft and a little blackened. Cool the capsicum in a plastic bag for a few minutes, then peel. Chop all the vegetables into small pieces and mix with the balsamic vinegar and remaining parsley and marjoram. Serve warm.

 Serve with barbecued or grilled (broiled) meat or chicken.

Chasseur Sauce

Serves 4

pan juices from pan-fried beef or veal steaks
50 g (1³/4 oz) butter
4 spring onions (scallions), finely chopped
200 g (7 oz/2¹/2 cups) button mushrooms, halved
170 ml (5¹/2 fl oz/²/3 cup) beef stock
2 teaspoons tomato paste (concentrated purée)
60 ml (2 fl oz/¹/4 cup) dry Madeira or white wine
2 teaspoons cornflour (cornstarch)
2 tablespoons chopped parsley

1   Set aside the frying pan containing the pan juices.

2   Heat the butter in a separate frying pan and cook the
    spring onion for 2 minutes. Add the mushrooms and cook
    for 5 minutes. Season with salt and pepper and set aside.

3   Add the stock and tomato paste to the pan containing the
    reserved pan juices and boil rapidly until reduced to 80 ml
    (2¹/2 fl oz/¹/3 cup). Combine the wine and cornflour and
    pour into the pan. Boil, stirring until slightly thickened. Stir
    in the mushrooms and parsley. Serve hot.

 Serve over pan-fried beef or
veal steaks.

Chilli Barbecue Sauce

Serves 4-6

20 g (³/4 oz) butter
1 teaspoon ground cumin
¹/2 teaspoon ground coriander
¹/2 teaspoon paprika
80 ml (2¹/2 fl oz/¹/3 cup) ready-made barbecue sauce
1 tablespoon sweet chilli sauce
2 teaspoons worcestershire sauce

1 Heat the butter in a small saucepan over low–medium heat. Add the cumin, coriander and paprika and cook for 30 seconds.

2 Add the barbecue sauce, sweet chilli sauce and worcestershire sauce and mix well.

 Serve with barbecued lamb, beef or hamburgers.

Chilli Dipping Sauce

Serves 4-6

1 tablespoon peanut oil

1 garlic clove, crushed

60 ml (2 fl oz/$^{1}/_{4}$ cup) sweet chilli sauce

2 tablespoons soy sauce

2 tablespoons sherry

1 tablespoon lemon juice

1   Heat the oil in a small saucepan over medium heat. Cook the garlic until just golden.

2   Add the chilli sauce, soy sauce, sherry and lemon juice and stir until smooth and heated through. Serve warm.

 Serve with Thai starters such as spring rolls and fish cakes.

Chilli Lime Dressing

Serves 6–8

60 ml (2 fl oz/¼ cup) lime juice
2 tablespoons fish sauce
1–2 teaspoons sambal oelek (chilli paste)
1 teaspoon sugar
60 ml (2 fl oz/¼ cup) oil

1 Combine the lime juice, fish sauce, sambal oelek and sugar in a small bowl.

2 Using a small wire whisk or fork, gradually whisk in the oil in a thin stream until well blended.

 Serve with chargrilled prawns (shrimp) or stir-fried Asian greens.

Chilli Mango Sauce

Serves 4

1 tablespoon oil
1 red onion, thinly sliced
3 garlic cloves, finely chopped
4 cm (1¹/₂ inch) piece ginger, finely chopped
2–3 red chillies, seeded and finely chopped
1 large mango, diced
1 tablespoon honey
¹/₄ teaspoon ground cinnamon
pinch of ground cardamom
pinch of ground cloves
pinch of freshly grated nutmeg
60 ml (2 fl oz/¹/₄ cup) dark rum
60 ml (2 fl oz/¹/₄ cup) lime juice
1 small handful coriander (cilantro) leaves, chopped

1　Heat the oil in a frying pan over medium heat. Cook the onion, garlic, ginger and chilli for 3–4 minutes, or until soft.

2　Add the mango, honey and spices and mix well. Cook until heated through, then reduce the heat and simmer gently for 5 minutes. Add the rum and simmer for 5 minutes.

3　Stir in the lime juice and coriander, and season. Serve warm.

 Serve with chicken or tuna.

Chilli Sauce

Serves 8

2 large red chillies
1 teaspoon ground cumin
400 g (14 oz) tin tomatoes
1 small red onion, chopped
1 garlic clove, crushed
125 ml (4 fl oz/^{1}/$_2$ cup) chicken stock
2 teaspoons red wine vinegar

1 Roast the chillies under a grill (broiler) or over a gas flame until the skin is black and blistered. Cool in a plastic bag, then peel the skin and remove the seeds and stems.

2 Put the ground cumin in a small, dry frying pan and fry for 30 seconds, or until fragrant.

3 Process the chilli, cumin, tomatoes, onion, garlic, stock and vinegar in a food processor until smooth.

4 Transfer the chilli mixture to a saucepan. Bring to the boil, then reduce the heat and simmer for 20 minutes. Serve warm or at room temperature.

 Serve with Mexican food.

Chinese Lemon Sauce

serves 4

60 ml (2 fl oz/1/4 cup) lemon juice
60 ml (2 fl oz/1/4 cup) chicken stock
1 tablespoon honey
1 tablespoon sugar
1/2 teaspoon grated fresh ginger
1 tablespoon cornflour (cornstarch)
2 spring onions (scallions), sliced on the diagonal
a few drops of sesame oil

1 Put the lemon juice, stock, honey, sugar and ginger in a saucepan with 125 ml (4 fl oz/1/2 cup) of water. Stir over medium heat until the sugar has dissolved.

2 Increase the heat and bring to the boil. Blend the cornflour with a little water and add to the pan, stirring constantly until the sauce boils and thickens. Remove from the heat, stir in the spring onion and season with salt. Drizzle with the sesame oil and serve warm.

 Serve with deep-fried won tons, spring rolls and dumplings. Also good with vegetables, chicken or fish.

Chunky Roasted Red Onion Sauce

serves 6–8

500 g (1 lb 2 oz) red onions, thinly sliced
1 kg (2 lb 4 oz) baby onions
3 large garlic cloves
2 tablespoons olive oil
1.5 kg (3 lb 5 oz) roma (plum) tomatoes, halved lengthways
1 teaspoon salt
3 tablespoons chopped oregano
440 g (15½ oz) tin tomatoes, roughly chopped
1 tablespoon muscatel liqueur or brandy
1 tablespoon soft brown sugar

1 Preheat the oven to 200°C (400°F/Gas 6). Put the red onion, baby onions and garlic in a large roasting tin with half the oil. Roll the onions in the oil so that they are lightly coated. Add the roma tomatoes, drizzle with the remaining oil and sprinkle with the salt and oregano. Roast for 1 hour.

2 Spoon the chopped tomatoes and juice into the roasting tin, taking care not to break up the roasted tomatoes. Drizzle the muscatel or brandy over the top and sprinkle with the brown sugar. Roast for 20 minutes. Serve hot.

 Serve with barbecued steaks and mashed potatoes.

Chunky Tomato Sauce

Serves 4

1.5 kg (3 lb 5 oz) tomatoes
1 tablespoon olive oil
1 onion, finely chopped
2 garlic cloves, crushed
2 tablespoons tomato paste (concentrated purée)
1 teaspoon dried oregano
1 teaspoon sugar

1   Score a cross in the base of each tomato. Place in a heatproof bowl and cover with boiling water. Set aside for 30 seconds, then transfer to cold water and peel the skin away from the cross. Finely chop the tomatoes.

2   Heat the oil in a saucepan over medium heat. Cook the onion, stirring, for 3 minutes, or until soft. Add the garlic and cook for 1 minute.

3   Add the tomato, tomato paste, oregano and sugar. Bring to the boil, then reduce the heat and simmer for 20 minutes, or until the sauce has thickened slightly. Season to taste.

 Serve hot with pasta, pan-fried steaks or veal schnitzel, or cool and use as a sauce for pizza bases.

Cocktail Sauce

serves 4-6

250 g (9 oz/1 cup) whole-egg mayonnaise
60 ml (2 fl oz/¼ cup) tomato sauce (ketchup)
2 teaspoons worcestershire sauce
½ teaspoon lemon juice
drop of Tabasco sauce

1 Put the mayonnaise, tomato sauce, worcestershire sauce, lemon juice and Tabasco sauce in a bowl and stir to combine. Season with salt and pepper.

 Serve with any cooked, cold prawns (shrimp) or shellfish.

Coconut and Chilli Dipping Sauce

Serves 6-8

2 teaspoons oil
2 teaspoons curry paste
1 small red chilli, roughly chopped
125 ml (4 fl oz/$^1/_2$ cup) coconut milk
1 teaspoon caster (superfine) sugar
1 teaspoon fish sauce
1 handful basil, chopped

1 Heat the oil in a small saucepan over low heat. Add the curry paste and chilli and stir for 30 seconds, or until heated through.

2 Add the coconut milk, sugar, fish sauce and basil and stir for 2 minutes. Serve warm.

 Serve with chunks of deep-fried fish or pieces of seafood.

Coriander Pesto

Serves 4

175 g (6 oz/2 bunches) coriander (cilantro)
2 garlic cloves, crushed
50 g (1³/4 oz/¹/3 cup) roasted macadamia nuts
1 teaspoon chopped red chilli
80 ml (2¹/2 fl oz/¹/3 cup) olive oil

1 Trim the roots from the coriander, leaving most of the stems. Wash and dry the stems.

2 Process the coriander, garlic, macadamia nuts and chilli in a food processor until finely chopped. With the motor running, add the oil in a thin stream until well combined. Season to taste.

 Serve with pasta, grilled (broiled) fish or chicken.

Corn and Chilli Salsa

Serves 4

4 corn cobs
oil, for brushing
1 small red onion, finely chopped
1 red capsicum (pepper), seeded and chopped
1 red chilli, seeded and chopped
2 tablespoons chopped coriander (cilantro) leaves
60 ml (2 fl oz/¼ cup) lime juice

1   Lightly brush the corn cobs with oil and sprinkle with salt and pepper. Cook under a hot grill (broiler) for 5–7 minutes, or until roasted, turning the corn so that it cooks all over. Set aside to cool, then slice the corn kernels from the cobs.

2   Put the corn kernels, onion, capsicum, chilli, coriander and lime juice in a large bowl and toss to combine.

 Serve with grilled (broiled) or barbecued steaks or chicken.

Cranberry Sauce

Serves 6–8

1 orange
500 g (1 lb 2 oz/4 cups) fresh or frozen cranberries
110 g (3³/4 oz/¹/2 cup) sugar
125 ml (4 fl oz/¹/2 cup) orange juice
2 tablespoons port
1 cinnamon stick

1 Peel the orange and cut the zest into thick strips, removing all the white pith.

2 Put the cranberries, sugar, orange juice, orange zest, port and cinnamon stick in a heavy-based saucepan. Bring to the boil, then reduce the heat and simmer for 5 minutes. Remove from the heat.

3 Remove the orange zest and cinnamon stick, including any small pieces that have broken away. Set aside to cool before serving.

 Serve with roast turkey, chicken or pork.

Creamy Horseradish Sauce

Serves 8–10

175 g (6 oz/$\frac{1}{2}$ cup) horseradish cream
1 bulb spring onion (scallion), finely chopped
60 g (2$\frac{1}{4}$ oz/$\frac{1}{4}$ cup) sour cream
125 ml (4 fl oz/$\frac{1}{2}$ cup) cream (whipping)

1   Combine the horseradish cream, spring onion and sour cream in a small bowl.

2   Whip the cream until soft peaks form. Fold the cream into the horseradish mixture. Season to taste.

 Serve with roast beef, smoked salmon or vegetable crudités.

Creamy Mushroom Sauce

Serves 4

30 g (1 oz) butter
pan juices from pan-fried beef, veal or chicken
350 g (12 oz/4^1/$_3$ cups) button mushrooms, sliced
2 tablespoons white wine
125 ml (4 fl oz/^{1}/$_2$ cup) chicken stock
125 ml (4 fl oz/^{1}/$_2$ cup) cream (whipping)
1 garlic clove, crushed
1 tablespoon snipped chives

1 Melt the butter in the frying pan containing the pan
juices over medium heat, add the mushrooms and stir for
5 minutes, or until the mushrooms are soft and golden.

2 Add the wine, stock, cream and garlic and bring to the boil.
Cook, stirring constantly, for 2 minutes, or until the sauce
has thickened slightly. Add the chives and serve immediately.

 Serve over pan-fried beef steaks,
veal steaks or boneless, skinless
chicken breasts.

Cucumber Dipping Sauce

Serves 6–8

1/2 Lebanese (short) cucumber, roughly chopped
1/2 carrot, chopped
2 spring onions (scallions), roughly chopped
1 small red chilli, seeded and chopped
1 teaspoon grated fresh ginger
1 tablespoon roasted unsalted peanuts
1 tablespoon chopped coriander (cilantro)
80 g (2³/₄ oz/¹/₃ cup) caster (superfine) sugar
185 ml (6 fl oz/³/₄ cup) white wine vinegar or rice vinegar

1   Briefly process the cucumber, carrot, spring onion, chilli,
    ginger, peanuts and coriander in a food processor until
    finely chopped, being careful not to overprocess the
    mixture. Transfer to a serving bowl.

2   Heat the sugar, vinegar and 60 ml (2 fl oz/¹/₄ cup) of water
    in a small saucepan. Stir until the sugar has dissolved, then
    pour over the cucumber mixture. Serve warm or cold.

Serve with Thai starters such as
spring rolls and fish cakes.

Cucumber and Ginger Salsa

Serves 4

2 Lebanese (short) cucumbers, peeled and diced

1 small red onion, finely chopped

2 tablespoons chopped pickled ginger

2 tablespoons chopped mint

1 tablespoon chopped coriander (cilantro) leaves

1 tablespoon fish sauce

1 tablespoon lemon juice

3 teaspoons sweet chilli sauce

1 teaspoon sesame oil

1 Put the cucumber, onion, ginger, mint and coriander in a bowl and mix well.

2 Add the fish sauce, lemon juice, sweet chilli sauce and sesame oil and toss to combine. Cover and refrigerate for at least 15 minutes before serving.

Serve with prawns (shrimp), smoked salmon, chargrilled trout fillet, salmon or tuna.

Cucumber Sauce

Serves 8

4 large cucumbers
2 tablespoons chopped capers
2 tablespoons chopped pickled gherkins (pickles)
2 tablespoons snipped chives
125 ml (4 fl oz/½ cup) cream (whipping)
2 tablespoons whole-egg mayonnaise
1 tablespoon white wine vinegar or tarragon vinegar
2 teaspoons dijon mustard

1   Halve the cucumbers lengthways and scoop out the seeds. Chop the flesh into 5 mm (¼ inch) cubes. Combine the cucumber, capers, gherkins and chives in a bowl.

2   Whisk together the cream, mayonnaise, vinegar and mustard. Add to the cucumber mixture and mix to combine. Season to taste. Cover and refrigerate the sauce for 30 minutes before serving.

 Serve with trout or salmon.

Cumberland Sauce

Serves 8

2 oranges
1 lemon
225 g (8 oz/³/₄ cup) redcurrant jelly
2 teaspoons dijon mustard
2 tablespoons red wine vinegar
250 ml (9 fl oz/1 cup) port

1   Remove the orange and lemon zest with a zester. Place the zest in a small saucepan with 250 ml (9 fl oz/1 cup) of water and bring to the boil. Cook for 5 minutes, then strain the liquid, reserving the zest.

2   Squeeze the juice from the oranges and lemon and pour into a saucepan. Add the redcurrant jelly, mustard, vinegar, port and reserved citrus zest. Slowly bring to the boil, stirring as the jelly melts. Reduce the heat and simmer gently for 15 minutes. Season to taste. Serve chilled or at room temperature.

 Serve this traditional sauce cold with ham, turkey, venison or game.

Curry Béchamel

Serves 4

250 ml (9 fl oz/1 cup) milk
1 slice of onion
1 bay leaf
6 peppercorns
30 g (1 oz) butter
1 small onion, finely chopped
2 teaspoons curry powder
1 tablespoon plain (all-purpose) flour
freshly ground white pepper

1 Put the milk, onion slice, bay leaf and peppercorns in a small saucepan. Bring to the boil, then remove from the heat. Set aside to infuse for 10 minutes, then strain the milk.

2 Melt the butter in a small saucepan. Add the onion and curry powder and cook, stirring, for 2 minutes, or until the onion is soft. Add the flour and cook, stirring, for 1 minute, or until the mixture is golden and bubbling.

3 Remove from the heat and gradually add the infused milk, stirring after each addition until completely smooth. Return to the heat and stir until boiling, then cook for 1 minute, or until thick. Season with salt and white pepper. Serve hot.

 Serve over steamed or poached fish.

Demi-glace

Serves 8

BEEF STOCK	ESPAGNOLE
1 kg (2 lb 4 oz) beef bones	2 tablespoons oil
1 tablespoon oil	2 carrots, finely chopped
1 onion, chopped	1 onion, finely chopped
2 carrots, chopped	1 celery stalk, finely chopped
5 parsley stalks	1 tablespoon plain (all-purpose)
2 bay leaves	flour
6 peppercorns	1/2 teaspoon tomato paste
	(concentrated purée)
	bouquet garni (see notes)

1 To make the beef stock, preheat the oven to 220°C (425°F/Gas 7). Roast the beef bones for 1 hour, or until browned. Heat the oil in a large saucepan and brown the vegetables, being careful not to burn them. Add the bones, parsley, bay leaves and peppercorns and cover with cold water. Bring to the boil, then reduce the heat and simmer for 3–4 hours, skimming off the fat as it rises to the surface. Add a little more cold water if needed. You should have about 875 ml (30 fl oz/3½ cups) of stock — if you have more, continue reducing; if less, add a little water. Strain and cool. Remove any fat that sets on the surface.

2   To make the espagnole, heat the oil in a saucepan and
    brown the vegetables. Add the flour and cook, stirring, until
    browned. Add 625 ml (21½ fl oz/2½ cups) of the beef
    stock with the tomato paste and bouquet garni and bring to
    the boil. Reduce the heat, half-cover the pan and simmer,
    skimming off any fat, for 30 minutes, or until reduced to
    250 ml (9 fl oz/1 cup). Strain and set aside to cool.

3   To make the demi-glace, put the espagnole and remaining
    beef stock in a saucepan and simmer until reduced by half.
    Strain thoroughly through a fine mesh sieve or muslin.
    Serve warm.

Notes: Don't use ready-made stock as it is far too salty for
this recipe. To make a bouquet garni, wrap the green part of a
leek around a bay leaf, sprig of thyme, some celery leaves and
a few stalks of parsely, then tie with string. To make a beef
glace, reduce the strained stock to a thick sticky liquid, which
will set to a jelly when cold. This gives a rich flavour when
added to sauces.

 Serve with any type of beef steak.

Dill Mayonnaise

Serves 6

185 g (6$^1/_2$ oz/$^3/_4$ cup) whole-egg mayonnaise
60 g (2$^1/_4$ oz/$^1/_4$ cup) plain yoghurt
$^1/_4$ teaspoon finely grated lemon zest
1$^1/_2$ tablespoons chopped dill
1 teaspoon lemon juice
pinch of caster (superfine) sugar

1 Put the mayonnaise, yoghurt, lemon zest, dill, lemon juice and sugar in a bowl and mix to combine. Season to taste.

2 Cover and refrigerate for 1 hour before serving.

 Serve with baked whole salmon.

Dill Sauce

Serves 6–8

125 g (4¹/2 oz/¹/2 cup) plain yoghurt
125 g (4¹/2 oz/¹/2 cup) sour cream
1 tablespoon horseradish cream
2 tablespoons chopped dill
3 spring onions (scallions), finely chopped

1 Combine the yoghurt, sour cream and horseradish in a bowl and stir until creamy.

2 Add the dill and spring onion and mix well. Season with salt and freshly ground black pepper. Serve chilled.

 Serve with fish, or spoon over steamed new potatoes.

Dried Apricot Sauce

Serves 8

250 g (9 oz/1¹/₃ cups) dried apricots
1 cinnamon stick
1 cardamom pod
90 g (3¹/₄ oz/¹/₃ cup) Greek-style yoghurt

1 Put the dried apricots, cinnamon stick and cardamom pod
in a saucepan and cover with cold water. Bring to the boil,
then reduce the heat and simmer for 15 minutes, or until
the apricots are very soft. Set aside to cool.

2 Remove the spices and purée the sauce until smooth,
adding more water if needed. Set aside to cool completely.

3 Stir the yoghurt into the sauce.

 Serve with a vegetarian nut roast.

Eggplant, Capsicum and Olive Salsa

Serves 6

1 eggplant (aubergine), diced
60 ml (2 fl oz/1/4 cup) olive oil
1/2 teaspoon salt
1 large red capsicum (pepper), seeded and diced
12 kalamata olives, pitted and finely chopped
4 spring onions (scallions), finely chopped
1 small red chilli, chopped
2 garlic cloves, crushed
2 teaspoons red wine vinegar
2 teaspoons lemon juice
1 tablespoon chopped parsley
2 teaspoons snipped chives

1   Preheat the oven to 180°C (350°F/Gas 4). Toss the eggplant
    with 2 tablespoons of the olive oil and the salt, then place
    in a single layer on a baking tray. Roast for 20 minutes, or
    until golden and cooked. Set aside to cool.

2   Combine the eggplant, capsicum, olives, spring onion, chilli,
    garlic, vinegar, lemon juice and remaining oil. Season to taste.
    Add the parsley and chives. Serve at room temperature.

 Serve with wood-fired bread or
barbecued beef, lamb or chicken.

Espagnole Sauce

Serves 8

40 g (1½ oz) butter
1 carrot, chopped
1 onion, chopped
1 celery stalk, chopped
1 tablespoon plain (all-purpose) flour
600 ml (21 fl oz) beef stock
1 teaspoon tomato paste (concentrated purée)
bouquet garni (see note)

1　Heat the butter in a saucepan over medium heat. Fry the carrot, onion and celery until soft. Add the flour and cook until brown.

2　Whisk in 400 ml (14 fl oz) of the stock and the tomato paste and add the bouquet garni. Bring to the boil, then reduce the heat and simmer, covered, for 30 minutes, skimming off any scum. Stir in the remaining stock. Strain the sauce before serving warm.

Note: To make a bouquet garni, wrap the green part of a leek around a bay leaf, sprig of thyme, some celery leaves and a few stalks of parsely, then tie with string.

 Serve with pan-fried or chargrilled steaks, barbecued meats or tuna.

Father's Favourite Sauce

Serves 8

5 large tomatoes (1 kg/2 lb 4 oz), chopped
1 large onion, chopped
125 ml (4 fl oz/$1/2$ cup) cider vinegar
185 g ($6^1/2$ oz/1 cup) soft brown sugar
60 ml (2 fl oz/$1/4$ cup) worcestershire sauce
1 teaspoon ground allspice
$1/2$ teaspoon ground ginger
$1/4$ teaspoon ground cloves

1 Put the tomato and onion in a large saucepan. Add the vinegar, sugar, worcestershire sauce and spices. Season with salt and pepper. Bring to the boil, then reduce the heat and simmer, stirring occasionally, for 40 minutes. Transfer to a bowl to cool.

2 Process the sauce in a food processor until almost smooth. Return to a clean saucepan and reheat until boiling. Set aside to cool slightly before serving warm.

 Serve with sausages, steaks or chops. Also good as a relish with cold meats.

Garlic and Lemon Dressing

Serves 4

2 tablespoons lemon juice
80 ml (2 1/2 fl oz/1/3 cup) oil
1 teaspoon wholegrain mustard
1 garlic clove
freshly ground white pepper

1 Whisk the lemon juice, oil and mustard in a small bowl until combined. Add the garlic clove and set aside to infuse for 30 minutes.

2 Remove the garlic clove and whisk again before serving. Season with salt and white pepper.

 Serve drizzled over a green salad.

Gazpacho Sauce

Serves 8-10

425 g (15 oz) tin tomatoes
1 Lebanese (short) cucumber
1 small red capsicum (pepper)
1 small green capsicum (pepper)
1/2 small onion, grated
2 garlic cloves, finely chopped
40 g (1 1/2 oz/1/2 cup) fresh breadcrumbs
2 tablespoons olive oil
2 tablespoons red wine vinegar
1 teaspoon sugar
1/4 teaspoon salt
1/4 teaspoon freshly ground black pepper

1 Drain and finely chop the tomatoes. Transfer to a large bowl. Halve the cucumber lengthways, remove the seeds and finely chop the flesh. Add to the bowl. Finely chop the capsicums, removing the seeds, and add to the bowl.

2 Add the onion, garlic, breadcrumbs, oil, vinegar, sugar, salt and pepper to the bowl and mix gently to combine. Cover and refrigerate for 30 minutes to let the flavours develop.

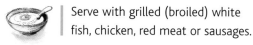 Serve with grilled (broiled) white fish, chicken, red meat or sausages.

Ginger Dipping Sauce

Serves 4–6

55 g (2 oz/¹/₃ cup) grated fresh ginger

2 tablespoons peanut oil

2 tablespoons sweet chilli sauce

1 teaspoon caster (superfine) sugar

1 tablespoon chopped coriander (cilantro) leaves

1 Combine the ginger, peanut oil, sweet chilli sauce, sugar and coriander in a small bowl.

 Serve with pieces of steamed or roast chicken or duck or with any Chinese-style dish.

Ginger and Sesame Dressing

Serves 8

1 teaspoon sesame oil

3 teaspoons rice wine vinegar

1 teaspoon finely grated orange zest

2 tablespoons orange juice

2 teaspoons grated fresh ginger

125 ml (4 fl oz/¹/2 cup) vegetable oil

1 Combine the sesame oil, vinegar, orange zest, orange juice and ginger in a small bowl.

2 Gradually whisk in the vegetable oil until well blended. Season with salt and freshly ground black pepper.

 Serve over mixed Asian salad greens or steamed Asian greens.

Gravy

Serves 8

pan juices from roast beef, lamb, chicken or pork
2 tablespoons plain (all-purpose) flour
500 ml (17 fl oz/2 cups) beef or chicken stock

1 Pour off any excess fat from the roasting tin. Sprinkle the flour over the pan juices and stir well, scraping any sediment from the bottom of the roasting tin. Place the tin on the stove over medium heat and cook, stirring, for 1–2 minutes.

2 Add the stock a little at a time, stirring well. Make sure the stock and the flour mixture are well combined before adding more stock, or the gravy will be lumpy. Bring to the boil and cook, stirring, for 1 minute, or until the gravy has thickened a little. Season to taste and serve immediately with the roast.

Note: The gravy may be strained to remove any dark flecks or meat particles.

Serve with roast beef, lamb, chicken or pork, and roast potatoes or Yorkshire pudding.

Green Goddess Dressing

Serves 6-8

375 g (13 oz/1¹/₂ cups) whole-egg mayonnaise
4 anchovy fillets, mashed
4 spring onions (scallions), finely chopped
1 garlic clove, crushed
3 tablespoons chopped flat-leaf (Italian) parsley
3 tablespoons finely snipped chives
1 teaspoon tarragon vinegar

1 Combine the mayonnaise, anchovies, spring onion, garlic, parsley, chives and tarragon vinegar.

 Serve as a salad dressing or with seafood.

Green Peppercorn Sauce

Serves 4

125 ml (4 fl oz/1/2 cup) chicken stock
pan juices from pan-fried steaks or chicken
125 ml (4 fl oz/1/2 cup) cream (whipping)
2 teaspoons tinned green peppercorns, rinsed and drained
2 teaspoons brandy

1   Pour the stock into the frying pan containing the pan juices. Stir over low heat until boiling, then add the cream and peppercorns. Boil, stirring constantly, for 2 minutes.

2   Add the brandy and boil for 1 minute more. Remove from the heat and serve immediately.

Serve with pan-fried steaks or boneless, skinless chicken breasts.

Grilled Tomato Salsa

Serves 4

4 large vine-ripened tomatoes
1/2 red onion, finely chopped
1–2 garlic cloves, crushed
1–2 small red or green chillies, seeded and finely chopped
3 tablespoons chopped coriander (cilantro) leaves
1 tablespoon olive oil
1 tablespoon lime or lemon juice

1 Cut the tomatoes in half and remove the seeds. Grill (broil) the tomatoes on a foil-lined tray until the skin is blistered and loose. Peel off the skin, cool and then chop the flesh.

2 Combine the tomato, onion, garlic, chilli, coriander, olive oil and lime or lemon juice in a glass or ceramic bowl. Season with salt and freshly ground black pepper. Set aside at room temperature for at least an hour before serving.

 Serve with barbecued or cold meats and vegetables.

Harissa Dressing

Serves 4–6

80 ml (2¹/₂ fl oz/¹/₃ cup) olive oil
2 tablespoons lime or lemon juice
2 teaspoons harissa
1 small garlic clove, crushed

1 Whisk the olive oil, lime or lemon juice, harissa and garlic
   in a small bowl until combined.

 Serve with couscous.

Herb Mayonnaise

125 g (4^1/$_2$ oz/^{1}/$_2$ cup) whole-egg mayonnaise

1 tablespoon chopped parsley

1 tablespoon snipped chives

2 teaspoons chopped capers

1 Combine the mayonnaise, parsley, chives and capers in a small bowl and mix well.

 Serve with fish patties or barbecued white fish fillets.

Herb Sauce

Serves 6

1 tablespoon finely chopped parsley
1 tablespoon finely chopped chervil
1 tablespoon finely shredded basil
finely grated zest of 1 small lemon
300 g (10^1/$_2$ oz/1^1/$_4$ cups) crème fraîche or sour cream

1   Put the parsley, chervil, basil, lemon zest and crème fraîche or sour cream in a bowl and mix to combine. Season with salt and freshly ground black pepper.

Serve with poached fish or chicken, or use as a filling for baked potatoes.

Herb Vinaigrette

Serves 4

2 tablespoons white wine vinegar
80 ml (2¹/2 fl oz/¹/3 cup) light olive oil
1 tablespoon finely chopped mixed herbs,
   such as tarragon, dill, chives or basil
1 teaspoon dijon mustard
freshly ground white pepper

1   Whisk the vinegar, olive oil, herbs and mustard in a small
    bowl until combined. Season with salt and white pepper
    and whisk until well blended.

 Serve drizzled over a green salad.

Herb Vinegar

Makes 1 litre (35 fl oz)

1 litre (35 fl oz/4 cups) white wine vinegar
3 tablespoons herbs, such as tarragon, dill, chives or basil
herb sprig

1 Combine the white wine vinegar and herbs. Pour into a
sterilized bottle and seal. Set aside for a week, shaking the
bottle occasionally.

2 Strain the vinegar into a clean sterilized bottle and add a
fresh herb sprig.

 Use in place of white wine vinegar
for a flavoured vinaigrette.

Hollandaise Sauce

Serves 4

175 g (6 oz) butter
4 egg yolks
1 tablespoon lemon juice

1. Melt the butter in a small saucepan. Skim any froth from the surface. Set the butter aside to cool.

2. Mix the egg yolks with 2 tablespoons of water in a small saucepan. Beat with a wire whisk for 30 seconds, or until the mixture is pale and foamy. Whisk over very low heat for 2–3 minutes, or until the mixture is thick and the whisk leaves a trail — do not let the pan get too hot or the egg yolks will scramble. Remove from the heat.

3. Add the cooled butter, a little at a time, whisking well after each addition. Try to avoid using the milky butter whey in the bottom of the pan. Stir in the lemon juice, season to taste and serve immediately.

Note: To prepare the hollandaise in a food processor, process the egg yolks, water and lemon juice for 10 seconds. With the motor running, add the cooled, melted butter in a thin stream.

 Serve with asparagus, egg dishes, poached salmon or chicken.

Horseradish Cream

Serves 6–8

150 ml (5 fl oz) thick (double/heavy) cream
2 tablespoons grated fresh or bottled horseradish
2 teaspoons lemon juice
pinch of sugar

1. Lightly whisk the cream, being careful not to overwhisk it as the acid from the lemon juice and horseradish will act as a thickener — if the cream is heavily whisked from the start, it may split.

2. Fold in the horseradish, lemon juice, sugar and a pinch of salt.

 Serve with smoked salmon or roast beef.

Japanese Dipping Sauce

Serves 10–12

125 ml (4 fl oz/^{1}/2 cup) lemon juice
125 ml (4 fl oz/^{1}/2 cup) dark soy sauce
1 tablespoon mirin
1 tablespoon sake
1 tablespoon dried bonito flakes
5 cm (2 inch) piece kombu seaweed

1 Whisk the lemon juice and soy sauce in a bowl. Add the mirin, sake, dried bonito flakes and seaweed and whisk until combined.

2 Refrigerate the sauce for 24 hours, then strain into a sterilized jar. Cover and refrigerate for up to two months.

 Serve with sashimi and sushi.

Japanese Sesame Miso Dressing

Serves 4–6

50 g (1³/₄ oz/¹/₃ cup) sesame seeds
1 teaspoon caster (superfine) sugar
2 tablespoons red or white miso
2 tablespoons mirin

1 Put the sesame seeds in a dry frying pan and fry over medium heat, stirring regularly, for about 5 minutes, or until lightly golden and aromatic. Immediately transfer the sesame seeds to a mortar.

2 Grind the sesame seeds until very finely crushed. Gradually incorporate the sugar, miso and mirin until the mixture forms a thickish paste.

Serve with blanched green beans, Asian greens or asparagus.

Leek and Caper Sauce

Serves 4

50 g (1³/4 oz) butter
1 leek, white part only, chopped
250 ml (9 fl oz/1 cup) white wine (riesling or chardonnay)
2 tablespoons capers, rinsed and squeezed dry
1 tablespoon chopped flat-leaf (Italian) parsley

1 Melt the butter in a saucepan and gently cook the leek until soft, but not brown.

2 Add the wine and simmer for 3–4 minutes. Stir in the capers and parsley and season to taste with salt and pepper. Serve immediately.

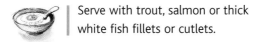 Serve with trout, salmon or thick white fish fillets or cutlets.

Leek and Pine Nut Sauce

Serves 6

2 leeks, white part only, finely chopped
1 onion, finely chopped
375 ml (13 fl oz/1¹/₂ cups) chicken stock
100 ml (3¹/₂ fl oz) dry white wine
6 egg yolks
125 ml (4 fl oz/¹/₂ cup) cream (whipping)
50 g (1³/₄ oz/¹/₃ cup) roasted pine nuts, roughly chopped

1 Put the leek, onion, stock and wine in a saucepan. Simmer, covered, for 15 minutes, or until the leek and onion are very soft.

2 Purée the leek mixture in a food processor, then pass through a sieve. Return to the saucepan and whisk in the egg yolks and cream.

3 Whisk over low heat for 2–3 minutes, or until the sauce is slightly thickened — take care not to let it boil or it will curdle. Stir in the pine nuts. Serve warm.

 Serve with veal cutlets, salmon, chicken, grilled (broiled) steaks or lamb or over mashed potato.

Lemon Grass and Lime Dressing

Serves 10-12

125 ml (4 fl oz/^{1}/2 cup) vegetable oil
125 ml (4 fl oz/^{1}/2 cup) lime juice
3 teaspoons sesame oil
2 tablespoons thinly sliced lemon grass, white part only
1 garlic clove, crushed
2 teaspoons soft brown sugar

1 Whisk the vegetable oil, lime juice, sesame oil, lemon grass, garlic and brown sugar in a bowl until combined. Season with salt and pepper and whisk to combine.

 Serve drizzled over mixed Asian salad greens.

Lemon, Lime and Thyme Vinegar

Makes 1 litre (35 fl oz)

2 limes
4 lemons
1 litre (35 fl oz/4 cups) white wine vinegar
20 thyme sprigs

1 Finely grate the zest of the limes and lemons. Squeeze the juice from the lime and two of the lemons.

2 Put the vinegar, lime juice, lemon juice, lime zest, half the lemon zest and half the thyme sprigs in a saucepan. Bring to the boil, then reduce the heat and simmer for 5 minutes. Remove from the heat and set aside at room temperature until cold.

3 Meanwhile, put the remaining lemon zest into a warm sterilized jar and add the remaining thyme sprigs. Strain the vinegar and pour it into the jar. Seal and store in a cool place for a week.

4 Line a funnel with muslin and strain the vinegar into warm sterilized bottles. Seal and label. Store for up to a year.

 Use in place of white wine vinegar for a flavoured vinaigrette.

Lemon Sauce

Serves 4

pan juices from pan-fried chicken
100 g (3¹/₂ oz) butter
2 tablespoons lemon juice
4 tablespoons shredded basil or parsley

1 Drain the excess fat from the pan containing the pan juices. Add the butter and cook over medium heat until the butter turns light brown.

2 Stir in the lemon juice and basil or parsley. Season lightly and serve immediately.

 Serve with pan-fried boneless, skinless chicken breasts.

Lemon Soy Dressing

Serves 6

2 tablespoons soy sauce
2 tablespoons rice wine vinegar
1 teaspoon honey
2 tablespoons lemon juice
1 teaspoon finely grated lemon zest
80 ml (2$^{1}/_{2}$ fl oz/$^{1}/_{3}$ cup) oil

1 Combine the soy sauce, vinegar, honey, lemon juice and lemon zest in a small bowl.

2 Gradually whisk in the oil in a thin stream until well blended. Season with freshly ground black pepper.

 Serve drizzled over mixed steamed green vegetables.

Lemon Thyme and Lime Dressing

Serves 8

170 ml (5¹/2 fl oz/²/3 cup) light olive oil
80 ml (2¹/2 fl oz/¹/3 cup) lime juice
2 tablespoons lemon thyme
1 teaspoon honey

1 Whisk the olive oil, lime juice, lemon thyme and honey in
a bowl until combined. Season with salt and freshly ground
black pepper and whisk well.

 Serve drizzled over a green salad.

Lime and Chilli Raita

Serves 4

3 handfuls mint, chopped
3 handfuls coriander (cilantro) leaves, chopped
1 teaspoon grated lime zest
1 tablespoon lime juice
1 teaspoon grated fresh ginger
1 jalapeño chilli, seeded and finely chopped (see note)
250 g (9 oz/1 cup) plain yoghurt

1 Combine the mint, coriander, lime zest, lime juice, ginger and chilli in a bowl.

2 Fold the yoghurt through the lime mixture. Season to taste with salt and freshly ground black pepper.

Note: Jalapeño chillies are smooth and thick-fleshed and are available both red and green. They are quite fiery and you can use a less powerful variety of chilli if you prefer.

Serve with chicken, seafood, chargrilled tuna, smoked or poached salmon, asparagus or artichokes.

Lime Mayonnaise

Serves 4-6

2 egg yolks
1 garlic clove, crushed
80 ml (2¹/₂ fl oz/¹/₃ cup) vegetable oil
80 ml (2¹/₂ fl oz/¹/₃ cup) olive oil
2 tablespoons lime juice
1 small green chilli, finely chopped

1   Put the egg yolks and garlic in a small bowl. Slowly add the vegetable oil, drop by drop, whisking continuously to form a smooth paste. When all the vegetable oil has been added, slowly add the olive oil in a thin stream while continuing to whisk.

2   Add the lime juice and chilli and mix well. Season to taste with salt and pepper.

 Serve with fried corn cakes.

Mandarin Sauce

Serves 8

310 g (11 oz) tin mandarin segments
2 tablespoons cornflour (cornstarch)
1 litre (35 fl oz/4 cups) chicken stock
125 ml (4 fl oz/$^{1}/_{2}$ cup) orange juice
2 tablespoons lemon juice
1 tablespoon honey
1 tablespoon soy sauce
2 teaspoons grated fresh ginger
1 tablespoon sugar

1 Process the undrained mandarin segments in a blender or food processor until smooth.

2 Put the cornflour in a small saucepan, add a little stock and stir until smooth. Add the remaining stock, orange juice, lemon juice, honey, soy sauce, ginger, sugar and mandarin purée. Stir over medium heat until the sauce boils and thickens. Serve hot.

  Serve with roast duck.

Mango Salsa

Serves 4-6

2 mangoes, chopped

3 spring onions (scallions), finely chopped

3 handfuls mint, chopped

1 tablespoon lime or lemon juice

1 Combine the mango, spring onion, mint, lime or lemon juice and some freshly ground black pepper in a glass or ceramic bowl.

2 Cover with plastic wrap and set aside for at least 15 minutes before serving at room temperature.

 Serve with chargrilled or barbecued meat, chicken or fish.

Mango Sauce

Serves 4

1 large mango, chopped
125 ml (4 fl oz/$^1/_2$ cup) coconut cream
1 tablespoon lime juice
2 teaspoons chopped mint

1 Process the mango, coconut cream and lime juice in a food processor until smooth.

2 Stir in the mint and season to taste with salt and freshly ground black pepper. Serve chilled.

 Serve with peeled, cooked prawns (shrimp).

Marsala Sauce

Serves 4

pan juices from pan-fried chicken
125 ml (4 fl oz/1/2 cup) dry Marsala
125 ml (4 fl oz/1/2 cup) chicken stock
80 ml (21/2 fl oz/1/3 cup) cream (whipping)

1   Drain the excess fat from the frying pan containing the pan juices. Add the Marsala and cook over medium heat for 1–2 minutes, using a wooden spoon to scrape the sediment off the base of the pan.

2   Add the stock and cream. Bring to the boil, then reduce the heat and simmer for 5–6 minutes, or until thickened and reduced. Strain the sauce to remove any sediment. Serve immediately.

 Serve with pan-fried boneless, skinless chicken breasts.

Mayonnaise

Serves 8–10

2 egg yolks
1 teaspoon dijon mustard
1 tablespoon lemon juice
185 ml (6 fl oz/³/4 cup) olive oil
freshly ground white pepper

1 Whisk together the egg yolks, mustard and lemon juice for 30 seconds, or until light and creamy.

2 Add the oil, a teaspoon at a time, whisking continuously. You can add the oil more quickly as the mayonnaise thickens. Season to taste with salt and freshly ground white pepper.

Note: To prepare the mayonnaise in a food processor, process the egg yolks, mustard and lemon juice for 10 seconds. With the motor running, add the oil in a slow, thin stream. Season to taste.

 Serve as a salad dressing or a sauce for fish or chicken dishes.

Melon Salsa

serves 6–8

1/2 honeydew melon, diced
1 red onion, finely chopped
2 small red chillies, seeded and finely chopped
3 tablespoons finely chopped coriander (cilantro) leaves
2 tablespoons lime juice

1 Combine the honeydew melon, onion, chilli and coriander in a large bowl.

2 Add the lime juice and mix well. Cover and refrigerate for 1 hour to let the flavours develop.

 Serve with chicken, white fish, squid, lobster, prawns (shrimp), pan-fried veal or pork.

Mint Raita

Serves 10

1 red onion, roughly chopped

1 green chilli, seeded and roughly chopped

3 cm (1¹/4 inch) piece ginger, chopped

3 handfuls coriander (cilantro) leaves

4 handfuls mint

2 tablespoons fish sauce

3 teaspoons caster (superfine) sugar

500 g (1 lb 2 oz/2 cups) Greek-style yoghurt

1 Process the onion, chilli, ginger, coriander, mint, fish sauce and sugar in a food processer until smooth.

2 Gently fold the yoghurt through the mint mixture just before serving.

 Serve with any Indian food, especially curries and tandoori chicken, or with seafood dishes such as chargrilled baby octopus.

Mint Sauce

Serves 4

80 g (2³/4 oz/¹/3 cup) sugar
2 tablespoons malt vinegar
4 tablespoons finely chopped mint

1 Put the sugar and 60 ml (2 fl oz/¹/4 cup) of water in a saucepan. Stir over low heat, without boiling, until the sugar has dissolved. Bring to the boil, then reduce the heat and simmer, without stirring, for 3 minutes. Remove from the heat.

2 Add the vinegar and mint to the sugar mixture. Cover and set aside for 10 minutes to let the flavours develop. Serve warm or cool.

 Serve with grilled (broiled) or roast lamb.

Mint and Teriyaki Dressing

Serves 6–8

1½ tablespoons mint
2 teaspoons dill sprigs
2 tablespoons lemon juice
125 ml (4 fl oz/½ cup) apple cider vinegar
½ teaspoon honey
60 ml (2 fl oz/¼ cup) teriyaki sauce

1 Process the mint, dill, lemon juice, vinegar, honey and
teriyaki sauce in a food processor until well combined.
Season to taste.

 Serve with salad greens or
chargrilled chicken.

Miso Sauce

Serves 6

2 tablespoons miso paste

1 egg yolk

2 teaspoons mirin

1 teaspoon sake

1 teaspoon rice wine vinegar

1 teaspoon English mustard powder

1 Whisk the miso paste, egg yolk, mirin, sake, vinegar, mustard powder and 4–5 tablespoons of water in a small heatproof bowl.

2 Place the bowl over a saucepan of gently simmering water and whisk until the mixture has thickened. Refrigerate until ready to serve.

 Serve with sliced sashimi tuna or salmon.

Mornay Sauce

Serves 4

330 ml (11^{1}/$_{4}$ fl oz/1^{1}/$_{3}$ cups) milk
1 slice of onion
1 bay leaf
6 peppercorns
30 g (1 oz) butter
1 tablespoon plain (all-purpose) flour
60 g (2^{1}/$_{4}$ oz/^{1}/$_{2}$ cup) finely grated cheddar cheese
^{1}/$_{4}$ teaspoon mustard powder

1 Put the milk, onion, bay leaf and peppercorns in a small saucepan. Bring to the boil, then remove from the heat. Set aside to infuse for 10 minutes, then strain the milk.

2 Melt the butter in a small saucepan and add the flour. Cook, stirring, for 1 minute, or until the mixture is golden and bubbling. Gradually add the infused milk, stirring after each addition until completely smooth. Continue stirring until the mixture boils and thickens. Boil for 1 minute more, then remove from the heat.

3 Stir in the cheese and mustard until the cheese has melted and the sauce is smooth. Season to taste. Serve hot.

Serve with grilled (broiled) lobster or oysters, steamed fish or vegetables.

Mustard Cream

Serves 8–10

90 g (3¼ oz/⅓ cup) dijon or wholegrain mustard
2 garlic cloves, crushed
250 g (9 oz/1 cup) sour cream
125 ml (4 fl oz/½ cup) cream (whipping)

1 Combine the mustard, garlic, sour cream and cream in a
bowl. Cover and refrigerate for 1 hour, then season well.

 Serve with hot or cold sliced
leg ham.

Mustard Mayonnaise

Serves 10-12

2 egg yolks
2 tablespoons wholegrain mustard
2 teaspoons dijon mustard
1 tablespoon white wine vinegar
250 ml (9 fl oz/1 cup) olive oil
1/2 teaspoon honey
1 tablespoon chopped tarragon, optional
freshly ground white pepper

1   Whisk together the egg yolks, wholegrain mustard, dijon mustard and half the vinegar for 30 seconds, or until light and creamy.

2   Add the oil, a teaspoon at a time, whisking continuously. You can add the oil more quickly as the mayonnaise thickens. Stir in the remaining vinegar, the honey and tarragon, if using. Season with salt and white pepper.

Note: To prepare the mayonnaise in a food processor, process the egg yolks, mustards and half the vinegar for 10 seconds. With the motor running, add the oil in a slow, thin stream. Stir in the honey, tarragon and remaining vinegar. Season to taste.

 Serve the mustard mayonnaise in place of plain mayonnaise.

Mustard Sauce

Serves 4-6

250 ml (9 fl oz/1 cup) chicken stock
6 spring onions (scallions), finely chopped
1 tablespoon white wine vinegar
2 tablespoons wholegrain mustard
250 g (9 oz/1 cup) sour cream

1 Combine the stock, spring onion, vinegar and mustard in a saucepan. Bring to the boil and cook for 5 minutes, or until the liquid has reduced by half.

2 Stir in the sour cream and heat through without boiling. Serve warm.

 Serve over pan-fried or grilled (broiled) pork, lamb or veal.

Nam Prik

Serves 4

60 ml (2 fl oz/¼ cup) fish sauce
1 tablespoon white vinegar
2–3 teaspoons finely chopped red chilli
1 teaspoon sugar
2 teaspoons chopped coriander (cilantro) stems

1 Combine the fish sauce, vinegar, chilli, sugar and coriander
in a small bowl. Stir until the sugar has dissolved.

 Serve as a dipping sauce with
Thai food.

Onion Gravy

Serves 4

1 tablespoon oil
6 onions, sliced
375 ml (13 fl oz/1¹/2 cups) beef stock
2 teaspoons cornflour (cornstarch)
2 teaspoons balsamic vinegar

1 Heat the oil in a large frying pan over low heat and cook
   the onion for 35–40 minutes, or until soft and beginning
   to caramelize.

2 Meanwhile, combine 1 tablespoon of the stock with the
   cornflour and stir to dissolve, ensuring there are no lumps.
   Add to the remaining stock with the vinegar.

3 Increase the heat and slowly add the stock mixture to the
   onion, stirring constantly until the mixture has thickened.
   Serve warm.

 Serve with grilled (broiled)
sausages and mashed potato.

Orange Hollandaise

Serves 4

175 g (6 oz) butter
4 egg yolks
2 tablespoons strained orange juice

1 Melt the butter in a small saucepan. Skim any froth from the surface. Set the butter aside to cool.

2 Mix the egg yolks with 2 tablespoons of water in a small saucepan. Beat with a wire whisk for 30 seconds, or until the mixture is pale and foamy. Whisk over very low heat for 2–3 minutes, or until the mixture is thick and the whisk leaves a trail — do not let the pan get too hot or the egg yolks will scramble. Remove from the heat.

3 Add the cooled butter, a little at a time, whisking well after each addition. Try to avoid using the milky butter whey in the bottom of the pan. Stir in the orange juice, season to taste and serve immediately.

 Serve with asparagus, egg dishes, poached salmon or chicken. Also good with steamed vegetables.

Orange and Mustard Vinaigrette

Serves 6–8

80 ml (2^1/2 fl oz/^{1}/3 cup) light olive oil
80 ml (2^1/2 fl oz/^{1}/3 cup) orange juice
^{1}/2 teaspoon finely grated orange zest
2 tablespoons vinegar
2 teaspoons wholegrain mustard

1 Whisk the olive oil, orange juice, orange zest, vinegar and mustard in a bowl until combined. Season with salt and pepper and whisk well.

 Serve drizzled over a green salad.

Orange and Parsley Dressing

Serves 6–8

1 tablespoon white vinegar
1 tablespoon cider vinegar
1 tablespoon red wine vinegar
1 tablespoon lemon juice
$1/2$ teaspoon salt
125 ml (4 fl oz/$1/2$ cup) orange juice
1 tablespoon honey
$1^1/2$ tablespoons dijon mustard
1 tablespoon finely chopped capers
1 sweet gherkin (pickle), diced
2 tablespoons chopped flat-leaf (Italian) parsley
60 ml (2 fl oz/$1/4$ cup) olive oil

1   Combine the vinegars with the lemon juice. Add the salt and whisk until dissolved.

2   Slightly heat the orange juice with the honey and stir to combine.

3   Pour the orange juice mixture over the vinegar mixture and add the mustard, capers, gherkin, parsley and olive oil. Season to taste with freshly ground black pepper. Serve warm or cold.

Serve as a warm or cold dressing for potato salad.

Orange Sauce

Serves 4

250 ml (9 fl oz/1 cup) duck or chicken stock
2 tablespoons shredded orange zest
170 ml (5^1/2 fl oz/^{2}/3 cup) orange juice
80 ml (2^1/2 fl oz/^{1}/3 cup) Cointreau or other orange liqueur
2 teaspoons cornflour (cornstarch)

1 Put the stock, orange zest, orange juice and orange liqueur in a saucepan. Bring to the boil, then reduce the heat and simmer gently for 5 minutes.

2 Blend the cornflour with 1 tablespoon of water and stir into the sauce until it boils and thickens. Serve hot.

 Serve with roast duck.

Papaya and Black Bean Salsa

Serves 4

1 small red onion, finely chopped

1 papaya (500 g/1 lb 2 oz), peeled, seeded and cubed

1 bird's eye chilli, seeded and finely chopped

1 tablespoon salted black beans, rinsed and drained

2 teaspoons peanut oil

1 teaspoon sesame oil

2 teaspoons fish sauce

1 tablespoon lime juice

1 tablespoon chopped coriander (cilantro) leaves

2 teaspoons shredded mint

1 Put the onion, papaya, chilli and black beans in a bowl and gently toss together with your hands.

2 Just before serving, whisk together the peanut oil, sesame oil, fish sauce and lime juice. Pour over the salsa and gently toss. Add the coriander and mint and serve immediately, at room temperature.

 Serve with chargrilled salmon or tuna steaks, chicken, beef or lamb.

Papaya Sauce

Serves 4

250 g (9 oz) papaya (see note)
60 ml (2 fl oz/¼ cup) cream (whipping)
1 tablespoon dry white wine
2 teaspoons wholegrain mustard
2 spring onions (scallions), finely chopped

1 Cut the papaya in half, discarding the seeds. Peel and finely chop the flesh and place in a bowl with all of the juices from the fruit.

2 Add the cream, wine, mustard and spring onion to the papaya. Season to taste with salt and pepper and whisk well. Cover and set aside for 20 minutes before serving.

Note: Slightly overripe papaya will give more flavour and juice.

 Serve with pan-fried pork or beef, lamb, chicken or turkey.

Parsley Béchamel

Serves 4

250 ml (9 fl oz/1 cup) milk
1 slice of onion
1 bay leaf
6 peppercorns
30 g (1 oz) butter
1 tablespoon plain (all-purpose) flour
3 tablespoons finely chopped parsley
freshly ground white pepper

1 Put the milk, onion, bay leaf and peppercorns in a small
   saucepan. Bring to the boil, then remove from the heat.
   Set aside to infuse for 10 minutes, then strain the milk.

2 Melt the butter in a small saucepan and add the flour.
   Cook, stirring, for 1 minute, or until the mixture is golden
   and bubbling. Remove from the heat and gradually add the
   infused milk, stirring after each addition until completely
   smooth. Return to the heat and stir until the mixture boils.
   Continue cooking for 1 minute, or until thick.

3 Remove from the heat and stir in the parsley. Season with
   salt and white pepper. Serve hot.

 Serve with fish or corned beef.

Parsley Pesto

Serves 4

200 g (7 oz/2 bunches) flat-leaf (Italian) parsley
2 tablespoons lemon juice
1 garlic clove, crushed
80 g (2³/4 oz/¹/2 cup) roasted blanched almonds
80 ml (2¹/2 fl oz/¹/3 cup) light olive oil

1 Place the parsley leaves in a food processor. Add the lemon juice, garlic and almonds and process until finely chopped.

2 With the motor running, add the olive oil in a thin stream until the mixture is well combined.

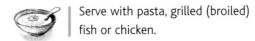 Serve with pasta, grilled (broiled) fish or chicken.

Peach and Basil Vinegar

Makes 425 ml (15 fl oz)

430 g (15¼ oz/2 cups) drained tinned peach slices
250 ml (9 fl oz/1 cup) white wine vinegar
2 large handfuls basil

1 Put the drained peach slices, vinegar and half the basil in a saucepan. Bring to the boil, then reduce the heat and simmer for 5 minutes. Remove from the heat and set aside at room temperature until cold.

2 Put the remaining basil in a warm sterilized jar. Remove the peach slices and basil from the vinegar and pour the liquid into the jar. Seal and set aside in a cool place for a week.

3 Line a funnel with muslin and strain the vinegar into warm sterilized bottles. Seal and label. Store for up to a year.

 Use in place of white wine vinegar for a flavoured vinaigrette.

Peach Salsa

Serves 4

1 tablespoon lime juice

2 teaspoons fish sauce

1–2 teaspoons sweet chilli sauce

2 peaches, peeled and cut into 1 cm ($^1/_2$ inch) cubes

1 small red onion, finely chopped

1 tablespoon chopped mint

1 tablespoon chopped coriander (cilantro) leaves

1 Put the lime juice, fish sauce and sweet chilli sauce in a bowl and mix well.

2 Add the peaches, onion, mint and coriander to the bowl and toss gently to combine. Cover and refrigerate for 30 minutes before serving.

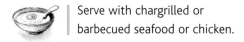 Serve with chargrilled or barbecued seafood or chicken.

Pesto

Serves 6

50 g (1³/₄ oz/¹/₃ cup) pine nuts
4 large handfuls basil
2 garlic cloves, crushed
35 g (1¹/₄ oz/¹/₃ cup) finely grated parmesan cheese
80 ml (2¹/₂ fl oz/¹/₃ cup) olive oil

1 Cook the pine nuts in a dry frying pan for 2–3 minutes, or until lightly browned. Transfer to a food processor and add the basil, garlic and parmesan. Process until finely chopped.

2 With the motor running, add the olive oil in a thin stream. Season if necessary.

 Serve with pasta, grilled (broiled) fish, chicken or tomatoes. Pesto can also be used as a spread on crackers and is ideal for finger food.

Pineapple Salsa

Serves 8

375 g (13 oz) pineapple, diced
1 small red onion, roughly chopped
1 red capsicum (pepper), seeded and chopped
1 jalapeño chilli, seeded
1 tablespoon grated fresh ginger
finely grated zest of 1 lime
1 tablespoon lime juice
1 handful coriander (cilantro) leaves, chopped

1 Process the pineapple, onion, capsicum, chilli and ginger in short bursts in a food processor until coarsely chopped.

2 Stir in the lime zest, lime juice and coriander. Season to taste with salt. Transfer to a small bowl, cover and set aside for 2 hours. Drain off any excess liquid before serving.

 Serve with grilled (broiled) fish or chicken.

Pistachio and Tarragon Vinaigrette

Serves 4

80 ml (2^1/$_2$ fl oz/^{1}/$_3$ cup) light olive oil
1 tablespoon pistachio oil
2 tablespoons white wine vinegar
1 tablespoon chopped pistachio nuts
1 tablespoon chopped tarragon
^{1}/$_4$ teaspoon sugar

1 Whisk the olive oil, pistachio oil, vinegar, pistachios, tarragon and sugar in a small bowl. Season with salt and pepper and whisk well to combine.

 Serve drizzled over a green salad.

Plum Sauce

Serves 4

1 teaspoon oil
1 garlic clove, crushed
310 g (11 oz/1 cup) dark plum jam
80 ml (2^1/$_2$ fl oz/^{1}/$_3$ cup) white vinegar
1–2 tablespoons bottled chopped chilli or sweet chilli sauce

1　Heat the oil in a small saucepan. Add the garlic and cook until just starting to turn golden.

2　Add the jam, vinegar and chilli or chilli sauce and stir over medium heat until well blended. Thin with a little warm water if necessary. Serve warm or at room temperature.

 Serve with pork or deep-fried crumbed calamari.

Ponzu Sauce

Serves 6–8

1¹/2 tablespoons rice vinegar
150 ml (5 fl oz) soy sauce
60 ml (2 fl oz/¹/4 cup) strained lemon juice
1 tablespoon mirin
100 ml (3¹/2 fl oz) dashi (see note)

1   Combine the vinegar, soy sauce, lemon juice, mirin and dashi. Cover and refrigerate overnight before serving.

Note: To make the dashi, dissolve ¹/4 teaspoon of instant dashi granules in 125 ml (4 fl oz/¹/2 cup) of boiling water and stir until dissolved.

 Serve with sashimi.

Prune and Cointreau Sauce

Serves 8

250 g (9 oz/1 cup) pitted prunes
250 ml (9 fl oz/1 cup) white wine
185 ml (6 fl oz/³/4 cup) orange juice
2 tablespoons Cointreau or other orange liqueur
20 g (³/4 oz) butter, chilled and cubed

1 Put the prunes, wine, 125 ml (4 fl oz/¹/2 cup) of the orange juice, half the liqueur and 60 ml (2 fl oz/¹/4 cup) of water in a saucepan. Bring to the boil, then reduce the heat and simmer for 10 minutes.

2 Remove from the heat and add the remaining orange juice and liqueur and 60 ml (2 fl oz/¹/4 cup) of water. Set aside to cool slightly.

3 Pass the sauce through a fine sieve into a clean saucepan. Heat before serving and whisk in the cubed butter, a few pieces at a time. The sauce will thicken slightly as the butter is added. Serve warm.

 Serve with roast pork.

Quick Satay Sauce

Serves 4-6

250 ml (9 fl oz/1 cup) pineapple juice
250 g (9 oz/1 cup) peanut butter
1/2 teaspoon garlic powder
1/2 teaspoon onion powder
2 tablespoons sweet chilli sauce
60 ml (2 fl oz/1/4 cup) soy sauce

1 Combine the pineapple juice, peanut butter, garlic powder, onion powder, sweet chilli sauce and soy sauce in a small saucepan. Stir over medium heat until the mixture is smooth and heated through.

2 Add a little water for a thinner sauce, if preferred. Reheat in a saucepan over medium heat before serving.

 Serve with grilled (broiled) or barbecued beef or chicken kebabs.

Quick Spiced Cranberry Sauce

Serve 4-6

250 g (9 oz/1 cup) whole cranberry sauce
1 teaspoon grated orange zest
60 ml (2 fl oz/1/4 cup) orange juice
1 teaspoon ground ginger
1/2 teaspoon ground cardamom
1/4 teaspoon ground allspice

1 Combine the cranberry sauce, orange zest, orange juice, ginger, cardamom and allspice in a small saucepan. Bring to the boil over medium heat, stirring occasionally.

2 Reduce the heat and simmer for 2 minutes. Set aside to cool to room temperature before serving.

 Serve with roast turkey, chicken or pork.

Raita (Cucumber Yoghurt Dressing)

Serves 4

250 g (9 oz/1 cup) plain yoghurt
1 garlic clove, crushed
1 small Lebanese (short) cucumber, grated
2 tablespoons chopped mint

1 Combine the yoghurt, garlic, cucumber and mint in a bowl. Season with salt and freshly ground black pepper.

 Serve with barbecued beef kebabs or Indian food.

Ranch Dressing

Serves 4

125 g (4$^{1}/_{2}$ oz/$^{1}/_{2}$ cup) whole-egg mayonnaise
125 g (4$^{1}/_{2}$ oz/$^{1}/_{2}$ cup) sour cream
2 tablespoons lemon juice
2 tablespoons snipped chives
freshly ground white pepper

1 Combine the mayonnaise, sour cream, lemon juice and chives in a bowl. Season with salt and white pepper and mix well.

 Serve with chicken wings.

Raspberry Vinaigrette

Serves 4

80 ml (2^1/$_2$ fl oz/^{1}/$_3$ cup) hazelnut oil
2 tablespoons raspberry vinegar
5 raspberries, finely chopped
^{1}/$_2$ teaspoon sugar
freshly ground white pepper

1 Whisk the hazelnut oil, vinegar, raspberries and sugar in a small bowl. Season with salt and white pepper and whisk to combine.

 Serve drizzled over a green salad.

Raspberry Vinegar

Makes 500 ml (17 fl oz)

290 g (10¼ oz/2⅓ cups) raspberries
500 ml (17 fl oz/2 cups) white wine vinegar
2 teaspoons caster (superfine) sugar
2–3 raspberries, extra, optional

1 Place the raspberries in a non-metallic bowl and crush gently with the back of a spoon.

2 Warm the vinegar in a saucepan over low heat. Add the vinegar to the raspberries and mix well. Pour the mixture into a sterilized glass bottle and set aside in a warm place for two weeks, shaking regularly.

3 Strain the vinegar through a muslin-lined sieve into a small saucepan. Add the sugar and stir over medium heat until the sugar has dissolved. Pour into the clean, warm, sterilized bottle. Add the extra raspberries, if using. Seal and label the bottle and store in a cool, dark place.

 Use in place of white wine vinegar for a flavoured vinaigrette.

Red Wine Gravy

Serves 6

pan juices from roast beef
2 tablespoons plain (all-purpose) flour
80 ml (2^1/$_2$ fl oz/^{1}/$_3$ cup) red wine
625 ml (21^1/$_2$ fl oz/2^1/$_2$ cups) beef stock

1 Drain off all but 2 tablespoons of the pan juices from the roasting tin. Place the tin on the stove over low heat. Sprinkle the flour over the pan juices and stir well, scraping any sediment from the bottom of the tin. Cook over medium heat, stirring constantly, for 1–2 minutes, or until the flour is well browned.

2 Combine the red wine and stock and gradually stir into the flour mixture, making sure the liquid is well incorporated after each addition. Heat, stirring constantly, until the gravy boils and thickens. Reduce the heat and simmer for 3 minutes, then season to taste with salt and freshly ground black pepper. Serve warm.

 Serve with roast beef.

Red Wine Sauce

Serves 4

30 g (1 oz) butter
pan juices from pan-fried beef steaks or lamb cutlets
1 small onion, thinly sliced
1 teaspoon plain (all-purpose) flour
2 teaspoons soft brown sugar
185 ml (6 fl oz/¾ cup) red wine

1 Melt the butter in the frying pan containing the pan juices over medium heat. Add the onion and cook, stirring, for 5 minutes, or until the onion is very soft. Add the flour and sugar and cook for 1 minute.

2 Gradually add the red wine, stirring constantly. Bring to the boil, then reduce the heat and simmer, stirring, for 5 minutes, or until the sauce has reduced by half. Season with salt and freshly ground black pepper. Serve warm.

 Serve over pan-fried beef steaks or lamb cutlets.

Redcurrant Sauce

Serves 4-6

2 tablespoons port
250 g (9 oz/³/4 cup) redcurrant jelly
1 cinnamon stick
grated zest of 1 lemon

1   Put the port, redcurrant jelly, cinnamon stick and lemon zest in a small saucepan. Simmer for about 5 minutes, stirring to dissolve the jelly. Strain and serve warm.

 Serve over venison steaks, lamb or chicken.

Remoulade

Serves 4

300 g (10½ oz/1¼ cups) whole-egg mayonnaise
1 tablespoon chopped capers
1 tablespoon chopped cornichons
2 anchovy fillets, chopped
2 teaspoons dijon mustard
2 teaspoons chopped chervil
1 teaspoon chopped tarragon

1 Put the mayonnaise in a bowl and add the capers, cornichons, anchovies and mustard.

2 Stir in the chervil and tarragon and season well.

 Serve with grated or chopped vegetables such as celeriac, carrots or potatoes.

Roasted Cashew Satay Sauce

Serves 10

250 g (9 oz/1²/₃ cups) roasted cashew nuts
150 g (5¹/₂ oz/1 cup) roasted peanuts
1 teaspoon cumin seeds
1 teaspoon coriander seeds
¹/₄ teaspoon fenugreek seeds
375 ml (13 fl oz/1¹/₂ cups) coconut milk
3 teaspoons kecap manis or thick soy sauce
2 teaspoons sweet chilli sauce
1 teaspoon soft brown sugar

1 Preheat the oven to 160°C (315°F/Gas 2–3). Roast the nuts
on a baking tray for 10 minutes, then set aside to cool.

2 Finely grind the cumin, coriander and fenugreek seeds with
a mortar and pestle. Fry over low heat in a dry frying pan,
shaking the pan regularly, for 3 minutes, or until aromatic.

3 Finely chop the nuts and spices in a food processor. Add the
coconut milk, kecap manis or soy sauce, sweet chilli sauce
and sugar and season to taste. Process until soft and chunky.

4 Transfer the sauce to a saucepan and gently heat through.
Serve warm.

 Serve with chicken or pork kebabs,
barbecued meats or sausages.

Roasted Corn and Avocado Salsa

Serves 6

2 corn cobs, husks removed
1 avocado, chopped
85 g (3 oz/½ cup) stuffed green olives, chopped
2 tablespoons finely chopped parsley
3 spring onions (scallions), shredded
1 tablespoon olive oil
2 tablespoons lemon juice

1 Cook the corn in a saucepan of boiling water for 5 minutes, or until just soft. Drain, cool and pat dry with paper towels. Using a large sharp knife, cut the kernels from the cobs and place in a single layer on a foil-lined tray. Cook under a very hot grill (broiler) for 10 minutes, or until golden brown, turning once to ensure even roasting. Set aside to cool.

2 Combine the corn, avocado, olives, parsley, spring onion, olive oil and lemon juice. Season liberally with salt and freshly ground black pepper. Toss well to make sure the avocado is coated with the dressing. Cover and refrigerate for 15 minutes before serving.

 Serve with pan-fried salmon, chicken, lamb or beef.

Roasted Pumpkin Sauce

Serves 4-6

500 g (1 lb 2 oz) pumpkin (squash)
2 tablespoons olive oil
2 garlic cloves, crushed
2 teaspoons cumin seeds
2 teaspoons coriander seeds
250 ml (9 fl oz/1 cup) vegetable stock

1 Preheat the oven to 200°C (400°F/Gas 6). Cut the pumpkin into wedges, leaving the skin on, and place in a roasting tin. Combine the olive oil and garlic and drizzle over the pumpkin. Season with salt and pepper. Roast for 1 hour, or until the pumpkin is tender. Set aside to cool slightly.

2 Fry the cumin seeds and coriander seeds in a dry frying pan for 5 minutes. Transfer to a food processor or mortar and pestle and process until ground.

3 Remove the skin from the pumpkin. Purée the pumpkin flesh, ground spices and stock in a food processor until smooth. Transfer to a saucepan and gently heat through.

 Serve with a vegetarian nut roast or roast beef.

Roasted Red Capsicum Salsa

Serves 6

2 red capsicums (peppers), seeded and quartered
2 tomatoes
1/2 small red onion, finely chopped
1–2 small red chillies, finely chopped
2 limes, peeled and segmented
2 tablespoons olive oil
1 teaspoon sugar

1 Preheat the oven to 180°C (350°F/Gas 4). Roast the capsicum in an oiled roasting tin for 30 minutes, turning regularly. If it begins to burn, add 2 tablespoons of water to the tin. Set aside to cool, then cut into small cubes.

2 Score a cross in the base of each tomato. Place the tomatoes in a heatproof bowl and cover with boiling water. Set aside for 30 seconds, then transfer to cold water and peel the skin away from the cross. Cut the tomatoes in half, scoop out the seeds and cut the flesh into thin strips.

3 Combine the capsicum, tomato, onion, chilli, lime segments, oil and sugar. Season with salt and freshly ground black pepper. Cover and set aside for at least 15 minutes.

 Serve with chargrilled lamb steaks, veal, beef, chicken, fish or seafood.

Roasted Red Capsicum Sauce

Serves 8

2 red capsicums (peppers), seeded and quartered
2 tablespoons olive oil
1 red onion, roughly chopped
1–2 garlic cloves, crushed
425 g (15 oz) tin chopped tomatoes
3 handfuls chopped parsley
1 large handful chopped basil
1 tablespoon tomato paste (concentrated purée)
1 tablespoon caster (superfine) sugar

1　Cook the capsicum, skin side up, under a hot grill (broiler) for 10 minutes, or until blackened. Cool in a plastic bag for 10 minutes, then peel away the skin and chop the flesh.

2　Heat the oil in a saucepan and cook the onion and garlic for 2 minutes, or until soft but not brown. Add the tomatoes, parsley, basil, tomato paste, sugar and 375 ml (13 fl oz/1½ cups) of water.

3　Add the capsicum and cook, stirring often, over very low heat for 45 minutes–1 hour, or until thick. Cool slightly, then purée in batches in a food processor. Season to taste. Serve warm.

 Serve with any grilled (broiled) meats or vegetables.

Roasted Walnut Sauce

Serves 8-10

300 g (10¹/2 oz/2¹/2 cups) walnut pieces
1 tablespoon extra virgin olive oil
¹/4 teaspoon paprika
2 slices white bread, crusts removed
300 ml (10¹/2 fl oz) milk
1 garlic clove, crushed
4 tablespoons roughly chopped parsley
125 ml (4 fl oz/¹/2 cup) light olive oil
25 g (1 oz/¹/4 cup) grated parmesan cheese

1   Preheat the oven to 190°C (375°F/Gas 5). Put the walnuts on a baking tray and toss with the extra virgin olive oil. Sprinkle with the paprika and a pinch of salt and toss well. Roast for 5 minutes, then set aside to cool.

2   Soak the bread in the milk until soft.

3   Process the walnuts, bread and milk mixture, garlic and parsley in a food processor until very fine.

4   With the motor running, slowly pour in the olive oil until the sauce is thick. Add the parmesan, season to taste and process briefly to combine.

 Serve with chargrilled vegetables.

Rocket Pesto

Serves 4–6

300 g (10^1/$_2$ oz/2 bunches) rocket (arugula)
1–2 garlic cloves, crushed
80 g (2^3/$_4$ oz/^{1}/$_2$ cup) roasted macadamia nuts
50 g (1^3/$_4$ oz/^{1}/$_2$ cup) finely grated parmesan cheese
125 ml (4 fl oz/^{1}/$_2$ cup) extra virgin olive oil

1 Put the rocket leaves in a food processor. Add the garlic, macadamia nuts and parmesan cheese and process until finely chopped.

2 With the motor running, add the olive oil in a thin stream until the pesto is thick and creamy. Season to taste.

 Serve with pasta, grilled (broiled) fish or chicken.

Rocket Salsa Verde

Serves 4

25 g (1 oz/1/3 cup) fresh breadcrumbs
125 ml (4 fl oz/1/2 cup) olive oil
2 tablespoons lemon juice
1 garlic clove, crushed
4 anchovy fillets, finely chopped
30 g (1 oz/3/4 cup) rocket (arugula) leaves, chopped
1 small handful flat-leaf (Italian) parsley, chopped
1 tablespoon capers, rinsed, squeezed dry and chopped

1 Combine the breadcrumbs, olive oil, lemon juice, garlic, anchovies, rocket, parsley and capers in a bowl. Season well with freshly ground black pepper.

2 Cover with plastic wrap and set aside at room temperature for 4 hours. Stir well just before serving.

Serve with pan-fried fish, meat or chicken. Also good as a pasta sauce.

Romesco Sauce

Serves 6–8

4 garlic cloves, unpeeled
1 roma (plum) tomato, halved and seeded
2 long red chillies
2 tablespoons blanched almonds
2 tablespoons hazelnuts
60 g (2¼ oz/⅓ cup) sun-dried capsicums (peppers) in oil,
   drained and chopped
1 tablespoon olive oil
1 tablespoon red wine vinegar

1 Preheat the oven to 200°C (400°F/Gas 6). Wrap the garlic in foil, put on a baking tray with the tomato and chillies and roast for 12 minutes. Spread the nuts on the tray and bake for 3–5 minutes. Set aside to cool for 15 minutes.

2 Blend the nuts in a blender until finely ground. Squeeze the garlic and scrape the tomato flesh into the blender, discarding the skins. Scrape the chilli flesh into the blender, discarding the seeds and skins. Add the capsicum, olive oil, vinegar, some salt and 2 tablespoons of water. Blend until smooth, adding more water, if necessary, to form a soft dipping consistency. Set aside for 30 minutes.

 Serve with grilled (broiled) fish.

Rouille

Serves 6

3 slices day-old Italian white bread, crusts removed
1 red capsicum (pepper), seeded and quartered
1 small red chilli, seeded and chopped
3 garlic cloves, crushed
1 tablespoon chopped basil
80 ml (2¹/₂ fl oz/¹/₃ cup) olive oil

1 Cover the bread with cold water and soak for 5 minutes.

2 Cook the capsicum, skin side up, under a hot grill (broiler) for 10 minutes, or until blackened. Cool in a plastic bag for 10 minutes, then peel away the skin and chop the flesh.

3 Squeeze the bread dry and place in a food processor with the capsicum, chilli, garlic and basil. Process until the mixture forms a smooth paste.

4 With the motor running, gradually add the olive oil until the mixture is the consistency of mayonnaise. Thin the sauce with 1–2 tablespoons of water. Season to taste with salt and freshly ground black pepper.

 Serve with fish and fish stews such as bouillabaisse.

Salsa Verde

Serves 4

3 handfuls flat-leaf (Italian) parsley
4 tablespoons mint
3 tablespoons dill
2 tablespoons snipped chives
1 garlic clove, crushed
1 tablespoon lemon juice
5 anchovy fillets
35 g (1¹/₄ oz/¹/₄ cup) capers, rinsed and squeezed dry
125 ml (4 fl oz/¹/₂ cup) olive oil

1 Process the parsley, mint, dill, chives and garlic in a food processor for 30 seconds, or until combined.

2 Add the lemon juice, anchovies and capers and process until combined.

3 With the motor running, slowly add the olive oil in a thin stream and process until the mixture is smooth.

 Serve with roast meats or grilled (broiled) fish kebabs or prawns (shrimp).

Sambal Oelek

Serves 6-8

200 g (7 oz/2¹/₂ cups) small red chillies
1 teaspoon salt
1 teaspoon sugar
1 tablespoon vinegar
1 tablespoon oil

1 Remove the stalks from the chillies. Put the chillies in a small saucepan with 250 ml (9 fl oz/1 cup) of water and bring to the boil. Reduce the heat and simmer, partially covered, for 15 minutes, then set aside to cool slightly.

2 Transfer the chilli mixture to a food processor and add the salt, sugar, vinegar and oil. Process until the mixture is finely chopped. Set aside to cool, then refrigerate in a sealed container for up to two weeks.

 Serve with rice and curries.

Satay Sauce

Serves 8

165 g (5³/4 oz/1 cup) roasted unsalted peanuts
2 tablespoons olive oil
1 onion, chopped
2 garlic cloves, crushed
3 cm (1¹/4 inch) piece ginger, grated
¹/2 teaspoon chilli powder
2 teaspoons curry powder
1 teaspoon ground cumin
400 ml (14 fl oz) coconut milk
50 g (1³/4 oz/¹/4 cup) soft brown sugar
1 tablespoon lemon juice

1   Process the peanuts in a food processor until finely chopped.

2   Heat the oil in a saucepan over medium heat and cook the
    onion for 5 minutes, or until softened. Add the garlic, ginger,
    chilli, curry and cumin and cook, stirring, for 2 minutes.

3   Add the coconut milk, brown sugar and peanuts. Reduce
    the heat and cook for 5 minutes, or until thickened. Add
    the lemon juice and season with salt. For a smooth sauce,
    process in a food processor for 30 seconds. Serve warm.

 Serve with beef or chicken kebabs
or with grilled (broiled) chicken.

Sesame Orange Dressing

Serves 4

1 teaspoon finely grated orange zest
2 tablespoons orange juice
80 ml (2$^1/_2$ fl oz/$^1/_3$ cup) vegetable oil
$^1/_4$ teaspoon sesame oil

1 Whisk the orange zest, orange juice, vegetable oil and
   sesame oil in a small bowl until well combined. Season
   with freshly ground black pepper.

 Serve with steamed English
spinach or other steamed greens.

Skordalia

Serves 6

2 large floury potatoes (500 g/1 lb 2 oz), chopped
5 garlic cloves, crushed
55 g (2 oz/^{1}/$_2$ cup) ground almonds
170 ml (5^1/$_2$ fl oz/^{2}/$_3$ cup) olive oil
2 tablespoons white wine vinegar

1 Boil the potatoes until tender; drain, then mash. Mash the garlic and almonds into the potato.

2 Gradually add the olive oil, mashing until smooth. Add the vinegar and season to taste. Mash well, adding 1 tablespoon of water at a time (you will need 3–4 tablespoons) to give a thick creamy consistency. Cover and refrigerate for up to a day. Serve cold.

 Serve with steamed beetroot and beetroot greens, fish croquettes, seafood, steaks, lamb or chicken.

Sorrel and Lemon Sauce

Serves 4

30 g (1 oz) sorrel
3 egg yolks
150 g (5¹/2 oz) butter, melted
60 ml (2 fl oz/¹/4 cup) lemon juice
freshly ground white pepper

1   Put the sorrel in a heatproof bowl, cover with boiling water and set aside for 30 seconds. Drain and refresh in cold water to keep the colour, then finely chop or tear the sorrel into very small pieces.

2   Put the egg yolks in a heatproof bowl and place over a pan of simmering water. Whisk the yolks for about 1 minute, or until they thicken.

3   Continue whisking and drizzle the melted butter onto the yolks, a little at a time, whisking after each addition, until thick and creamy. Remove the bowl from the heat.

4   Whisk in the lemon juice and sorrel and season to taste with salt and white pepper. Serve warm.

 Serve with chicken, grilled (broiled) salmon or other fish.

Soubise (Onion Sauce)

Serves 4–6

50 g (1³/₄ oz) butter
1 large onion (200 g/7 oz), very finely chopped
250 ml (9 fl oz/1 cup) milk
1 onion, sliced, extra
3 peppercorns
1 bay leaf
1 tablespoon plain (all-purpose) flour
60 ml (2 fl oz/¹/₄ cup) cream (whipping)

1 Heat 30 g (1 oz) of the butter in a frying pan. Add the finely chopped onion and cook over low–medium heat until soft and translucent but not brown.

2 Put the milk, sliced onion, peppercorns and bay leaf in a small saucepan. Bring to the boil, then remove from the heat and set aside to infuse.

3 Melt the remaining butter in a saucepan over low heat. Stir in the flour and cook for 1 minute, or until foaming. Remove from the heat and strain in the milk, whisking thoroughly. Return to the heat and bring to the boil, whisking until thick. Season to taste. Reduce the heat and simmer for 2 minutes. Stir in the chopped onion and cream. Serve warm.

 Serve with cooked meats.

Sour Cherry Sauce

Serves 6

680 g (1 lb 8 oz) jar pitted morello (sour) cherries
80 ml (2$^{1}/_{2}$ fl oz/$^{1}/_{3}$ cup) port
1 teaspoon dijon mustard
$^{1}/_{2}$ teaspoon grated orange zest
60 ml (2 fl oz/$^{1}/_{4}$ cup) strained orange juice
1 chicken stock cube
1 tablespoon cornflour (cornstarch)

1   Drain the cherries, reserving 250 ml (9 fl oz/1 cup) of the liquid. Place the liquid in a saucepan with the port, mustard, orange zest and orange juice. Crumble in the stock cube and bring to the boil.

2   Blend the cornflour with 2 tablespoons of water and stir into the sauce. Bring to the boil and add the drained cherries, then reduce the heat and simmer, stirring occasionally, for 5 minutes. Season to taste and serve hot.

 Serve with roast duck, turkey, pork, ham, smoked chicken or any type of poultry or game.

Soy and Sesame Dipping Sauce

Serves 8

250 ml (9 fl oz/1 cup) rice vinegar or white wine vinegar

115 g (4 oz/¹/2 cup) caster (superfine) sugar

2 tablespoons dark soy sauce

¹/4 teaspoon salt

1 tablespoon sesame seeds, roasted

1 tablespoon honey

1 Combine the vinegar and sugar in a small saucepan. Stir over low heat until the sugar has dissolved.

2 Transfer the sugar mixture to a serving bowl and add the soy sauce, salt, sesame seeds and honey. Serve warm.

 Serve with Thai or Chinese starters. Also good with fried or steamed chicken or fish.

Spiced Coconut Sauce

Serves 2-4

40 g (1¹/₂ oz/¹/₂ small bunch) coriander (cilantro)
2 teaspoons oil
3 cm (1¹/₄ inch) piece ginger, grated
2 lemon grass stems, white part only, finely chopped
2 small red chillies, finely chopped
1 garlic clove, finely chopped
60–100 ml (2–3¹/₂ fl oz) coconut cream
2 tablespoons rice vinegar
1 teaspoon soft brown sugar

1 Finely chop the coriander, keeping the roots, stems and leaves separate. Heat the oil in a frying pan over low heat and cook the coriander root, ginger, lemon grass, chilli and garlic, stirring constantly, for 3 minutes, or until aromatic.

2 Stir in 60 ml (2 fl oz/¹/₄ cup) of the coconut cream. Increase the heat to high and bring the sauce to a rapid boil. Cook for about 1 minute, or until the mixture looks oily. Add the remaining coconut cream if the sauce becomes too thick.

3 Transfer the mixture to a bowl and stir in the coriander stems and leaves, vinegar and brown sugar. Add salt and more sugar, to taste. Serve at room temperature.

 Serve with baked whole fish or chicken.

Strawberry Vinaigrette

Serves 6

80 ml (2¹/₂ fl oz/¹/₃ cup) light olive oil
2 tablespoons strawberry vinegar
¹/₂ teaspoon dijon mustard
¹/₂ teaspoon sugar

1 Whisk the olive oil, vinegar, mustard and sugar in a small bowl. Season with salt and freshly ground black pepper and whisk well.

 Serve drizzled over a green salad.

Sun-dried Tomato Pesto

Serves 6

150 g (5$^{1}/_{2}$ oz/1 cup) sun-dried tomatoes
1 garlic clove, crushed
25 g (1 oz/$^{1}/_{4}$ cup) walnuts
25 g (1 oz/$^{1}/_{4}$ cup) parmesan cheese
80 ml (2$^{1}/_{2}$ fl oz/$^{1}/_{3}$ cup) olive oil

1   Soak the sun-dried tomatoes in boiling water for a few minutes until soft. Drain and squeeze out the excess water.

2   Process the soaked tomatoes, garlic, walnuts and parmesan in a food processor until finely chopped.

3   With the motor running, add the olive oil in a thin stream until well combined. Season with salt and freshly ground black pepper.

 Serve with pasta, grilled (broiled) fish or chicken.

Sweet Chilli Dressing

serves 4–6

1 red chilli, finely chopped
60 ml (2 fl oz/¼ cup) lemon juice
2 tablespoons soft brown sugar
2 tablespoons finely chopped coriander (cilantro) leaves
1 tablespoon fish sauce
1 tablespoon sweet chilli sauce

1 Whisk the chilli, lemon juice, brown sugar, coriander, fish sauce and sweet chilli sauce in a small bowl until well combined.

 Serve drizzled over chargrilled baby octopus.

Sweet Chilli Sauce

Serves 4-6

125 ml (4 fl oz/¹/2 cup) white wine vinegar
165 g (5³/4 oz/³/4 cup) sugar
4 red chillies, roughly chopped

1. Put the vinegar, sugar, chilli and a pinch of salt in a small saucepan. Heat, stirring, without boiling, until the sugar has completely dissolved. Bring to the boil, then reduce the heat and simmer for 10 minutes. Set aside to cool.

2. Transfer the cooled chilli mixture to a food processor and process until the chilli is finely chopped.

 Serve with Thai starters such as spring rolls and fish cakes.

Sweet and Sour Sauce

Serves 6–8

2 tablespoons dry sherry
250 ml (9 fl oz/1 cup) pineapple juice
60 ml (2 fl oz/¼ cup) white wine vinegar
2 teaspoons soy sauce
2 tablespoons soft brown sugar
2 tablespoons tomato sauce (ketchup)
1 small red capsicum (pepper), seeded and finely diced
1 tablespoon cornflour (cornstarch)

1 Combine the sherry, pineapple juice, vinegar, soy sauce, brown sugar and tomato sauce in a saucepan. Stir over low heat until the sugar has dissolved. Bring to the boil and add the capsicum.

2 Mix the cornflour with 1 tablespoon of water. Add to the saucepan and cook, stirring, until the mixture boils and thickens. Reduce the heat and simmer for 2 minutes. Serve immediately.

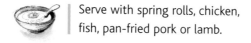 Serve with spring rolls, chicken, fish, pan-fried pork or lamb.

Tahini Dressing

Serves 4–6

2 tablespoons tahini

3 teaspoons lemon juice

1 small garlic clove, crushed

2 tablespoons sour cream

1 tablespoon chopped parsley

1 Put the tahini, lemon juice, garlic, sour cream, parsley and a pinch of salt in a small bowl and stir to combine. Add 2–3 tablespoons of water and stir until creamy.

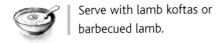

Serve with lamb koftas or barbecued lamb.

Tarragon Mayonnaise

Serves 4

1 egg yolk
1 tablespoon tarragon vinegar
$1/2$ teaspoon dijon mustard
170 ml ($5^{1}/_{2}$ fl oz/$^{2}/_{3}$ cup) olive oil
freshly ground white pepper

1 Put the egg yolk, vinegar and mustard in a bowl and beat with a wire whisk for 1 minute.

2 Add the oil, 1 teaspoon at a time, whisking constantly until the mixture is thick and creamy. As the mixture thickens, add the oil in a thin, steady stream. Season to taste with salt and white pepper.

 Serve with steamed artichokes.

Tarragon Vinegar

Makes 500 ml (17 fl oz)

500 ml (17 fl oz/2 cups) white wine vinegar
1 handful tarragon
1 tarragon sprig, extra

1 Heat the vinegar in a saucepan over low heat.

2 Gently bruise the tarragon in your hands and put into a
   500 ml (17 fl oz/2 cup) sterilized glass bottle.

3 Pour the vinegar into the bottle, seal with a non-metallic
   lid and shake well. Leave the vinegar to infuse in a warm
   place for two weeks.

4 Strain the vinegar and return to the clean, warm, sterilized
   bottle. Add the tarragon sprig, then seal and label. Store in
   a cool, dark place.

 Use in place of white wine vinegar
for a flavoured vinaigrette.

Tartare Sauce

Serves 8

375 g (13 oz/1½ cups) whole-egg mayonnaise
1 tablespoon finely chopped onion
1 teaspoon lemon juice
1 tablespoon chopped gherkins (pickles)
1 teaspoon chopped capers
¼ teaspoon dijon mustard
1 tablespoon finely chopped parsley

1 Put the mayonnaise, onion, lemon juice, gherkins, capers, mustard and parsley in a bowl. Mix well and season with salt and pepper.

 Serve with deep-fried battered or crumbed fish or calamari rings.

Thai Spicy Dipping Sauce

Serves 4

2 spring onions (scallions), finely chopped
1 teaspoon chilli powder
1 tablespoon lime or lemon juice
1 tablespoon fish sauce
1 teaspoon sugar

1 Combine the spring onion, chilli powder, lime or lemon juice, fish sauce and sugar in a glass or ceramic bowl.

 Serve with Thai pork, beef or chicken dishes.

Thousand Island Dressing

Serves 6

125 g (4$^{1}/_{2}$ oz/$^{1}/_{2}$ cup) whole-egg mayonnaise
1 tablespoon tomato paste (concentrated purée)
1 teaspoon dijon mustard
2 teaspoons malt vinegar
freshly ground white pepper

1 Put the mayonnaise, tomato paste, mustard and vinegar in a small bowl. Stir until well combined. Season to taste with salt and white pepper.

 Serve drizzled over a green salad.

Tomato and Chilli Sauce

Serves 4–6

1 kg (2 lb 4 oz) tomatoes
1 tablespoon olive oil
1 onion, finely chopped
2–3 garlic cloves, crushed
1–2 small red chillies, finely chopped
2 teaspoons grated fresh ginger
185 g (6^1/2 oz/1 cup) soft brown sugar
1 large handful basil, chopped
250 ml (9 fl oz/1 cup) red wine vinegar
80 ml (2^1/2 fl oz/^{1}/3 cup) dry sherry

1 Score a cross in the base of each tomato. Place in a heatproof bowl and cover with boiling water. Set aside for 30 seconds, then transfer to cold water and peel the skin away from the cross. Cut the tomatoes in half, scoop out the seeds and chop the flesh.

2 Heat the oil in a large saucepan and cook the onion, garlic, chilli and ginger, stirring, for 2 minutes, without browning. Add the tomato, sugar, basil, vinegar and sherry. Cook over low heat, stirring often, for 1 hour, or until thick and syrupy. Serve hot or cold.

 Serve with meat, chicken, fish, seafood or vegetables.

Tomato Salsa

Serves 6

4 roma (plum) tomatoes
1 red onion, finely chopped
1 bird's eye chilli, seeded and thinly sliced
3 tablespoons chopped coriander (cilantro) leaves
1–2 tablespoons lime juice
1/2 teaspoon salt

1 Cut the tomatoes in half horizontally and scoop out the seeds. Finely chop the tomato flesh and place it in a bowl.

2 Add the onion, chilli, coriander, lime juice and salt to the tomato and toss gently to combine. Cover and refrigerate for 1 hour before serving.

 Serve with chicken, seafood, grilled (broiled) meats or Mexican food.

Tomato Sauce

Serves 4

1 tablespoon olive oil
20 g (3/4 oz) butter
1 small onion, finely chopped
1 garlic clove, crushed
1–2 teaspoons Italian dried mixed herbs
2 large tomatoes, chopped
125 ml (4 fl oz/1/2 cup) tomato passata (puréed tomatoes)
2 teaspoons balsamic vinegar

1 Heat the oil and butter in a small saucepan. Add the onion, garlic and mixed herbs and cook for 2–3 minutes, or until the onion is soft.

2 Stir in the tomato, tomato passata and vinegar and cook for 3–4 minutes. Set aside to cool slightly.

3 Process the tomato mixture in a food processor until smooth. Season to taste with salt and freshly ground black pepper. Serve warm or cold.

 Serve with hamburgers, sausages, steaks or fish.

Velouté Sauce

Serves 4

30 g (1 oz) butter
30 g (1 oz/¼ cup) plain (all-purpose) flour
375 ml (13 fl oz/1½ cups) chicken, fish or veal stock
lemon juice, to taste
1 tablespoon cream (whipping)

1 Melt the butter in a saucepan over medium heat, add the flour and cook, without browning, for 2 minutes, or until a thick paste has formed.

2 Whisk in the stock a little at a time to prevent the mixture from becoming lumpy. Cook, whisking continuously, for 3–5 minutes, or until the sauce is quite thick and doesn't have a floury taste.

3 Season to taste with salt, freshly ground black pepper and lemon juice, adding a little at a time. Stir in the cream and serve immediately, as the sauce will quickly thicken. If necessary, add a little extra stock to thin it down.

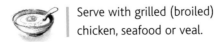 Serve with grilled (broiled) chicken, seafood or veal.

Vinaigrette (French Dressing)

Serves 4

2 tablespoons white wine vinegar
80 ml (2¹/₂ fl oz/¹/₃ cup) light olive oil
1 teaspoon dijon mustard

1 Whisk the vinegar, olive oil and mustard in a small bowl until combined. Season with salt and freshly ground black pepper and whisk until well blended.

 Serve drizzled over a green salad.

Wasabi Mayonnaise

Serves 4

125 g (4^1/2 oz/^{1}/2 cup) whole-egg mayonnaise
1 teaspoon wasabi paste
2 teaspoons Japanese soy sauce

1 Put the mayonnaise, wasabi paste and soy sauce in a small bowl and stir to combine. Cover and refrigerate until ready to serve.

 Serve with chicken or seafood.

Yakitori Sauce

Serves 6

125 ml (4 fl oz/$\frac{1}{2}$ cup) sake
125 ml (4 fl oz/$\frac{1}{2}$ cup) mirin
185 ml (6 fl oz/$\frac{3}{4}$ cup) Japanese soy sauce
2 tablespoons sugar

1 Put the sake, mirin, soy sauce and sugar in a saucepan and stir over low heat until the sugar has dissolved. Bring to the boil, then remove from the heat.

 Brush the sauce over chicken or fish skewers as they are cooking.

Crème Anglaise Chocolate Fudge Sauce R

Sweet

berry Coulis Zabaglione Brandy Custard

Apricot Liqueur Sauce

Serves 6

125 g (4¹/₂ oz/²/₃ cup) dried apricots, roughly chopped
250 ml (9 fl oz/1 cup) apple juice
3 wide strips lemon zest, white pith removed
55 g (2 oz/¹/₄ cup) sugar
1 tablespoon Cointreau or other orange liqueur, optional

1 Put the apricots, apple juice, lemon zest and 250 ml
(9 fl oz/1 cup) of water in a saucepan. Bring to the boil,
then reduce the heat and simmer, partially covered, for
10 minutes, or until the apricots are tender. Remove the
lemon zest.

2 Add the sugar and stir until it has dissolved completely.
Set aside to cool for 10 minutes.

3 Transfer the apricot mixture to a food processor and
process until smooth. Stir in the liqueur, if using.

 Serve with steamed puddings.

Berry Coulis

Serves 6

250 g (9 oz/2 cups) mixed berries, such as strawberries,
  raspberries and blackberries
2–4 tablespoons icing (confectioners') sugar, or to taste
1 tablespoon lemon juice
1–2 tablespoons Cointreau or other orange liqueur, optional

1 Hull the berries and place in a food processor.

2 Add the sugar and lemon juice and process until smooth.
   Stir in the liqueur, if using.

 Serve with fresh or poached fruit,
soufflés, ice cream, sorbet, pies
and tarts.

Berry Sauce

Serves 4-6

300 g (10$^{1}/_{2}$ oz/2$^{1}/_{3}$ cups) mixed raspberries and blackberries
250 g (9 oz/1$^{2}/_{3}$ cups) hulled and halved strawberries
1 tablespoon sugar
$^{1}/_{2}$ teaspoon grated lemon zest

1. Put the raspberries, blackberries and strawberries in a saucepan. Gently stir over low heat until heated through.

2. Add the sugar and lemon zest and stir until the sugar has dissolved and the liquid is syrupy. Serve warm.

 Serve with vanilla ice cream.

Blackberry Sauce

Serves 4

150 g (5 1/2 oz/1 1/4 cups) blackberries
80 ml (2 1/2 fl oz/1/3 cup) red wine
2 tablespoons caster (superfine) sugar
1 teaspoon cornflour (cornstarch)

1 Put the blackberries, wine and sugar in a small saucepan. Stir over low heat until the sugar has dissolved, pressing the berries with the back of a spoon, then simmer for 2 minutes.

2 Blend the cornflour with 2 teaspoons of water, add to the saucepan and stir until the mixture boils and thickens. Strain the sauce to remove the seeds. Set aside to cool before serving.

 Serve with mousse or vanilla ice cream.

Blueberry Sauce

Serves 6

500 g (1 lb 2 oz/3¼ cups) blueberries
2 tablespoons balsamic vinegar
55 g (2 oz/¼ cup) caster (superfine) sugar

1 Combine the blueberries and vinegar in a non-metallic bowl and set aside for 30 minutes to macerate the fruit.

2 Transfer the blueberry mixture to a saucepan and add the sugar. Stir over low heat until the sugar has dissolved. Bring to the boil, then reduce the heat and simmer for 2–3 minutes. Serve warm.

 Serve with ice cream or pancakes.

Brandy Cream Sauce

Serves 12

2 eggs, separated
80 g (2³/4 oz/¹/3 cup) caster (superfine) sugar
80 ml (2¹/2 fl oz/¹/3 cup) brandy
250 ml (9 fl oz/1 cup) cream (whipping), lightly whipped

1 Beat the egg yolks and sugar until the mixture is thick and creamy and the sugar has dissolved. Stir in the brandy and fold in the cream.

2 Beat the egg whites in a small bowl until soft peaks form. Fold into the sauce and serve immediately.

 Serve with plum pudding or chocolate steamed pudding, fresh or poached fruit or fruit pies.

Brandy Custard

Serves 6–8

3 egg yolks
115 g (4 oz/1/2 cup) caster (superfine) sugar
1 tablespoon custard powder
250 ml (9 fl oz/1 cup) milk
250 ml (9 fl oz/1 cup) cream (whipping)
2 tablespoons brandy

1 Whisk the egg yolks, sugar and custard powder in a bowl.

2 Combine the milk and cream in a saucepan and heat until just boiling. Gradually pour onto the egg yolk mixture, whisking continuously.

3 Transfer the mixture to the saucepan and stir over low heat for 5 minutes, or until the custard has thickened. Stir in the brandy. Serve warm.

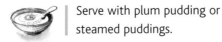 Serve with plum pudding or steamed puddings.

Burnt Sugar Sauce

Serves 6

440 g (15½ oz/2 cups) sugar

1 Mix the sugar and 250 ml (9 fl oz/1 cup) of water in a deep saucepan. Stir over low heat, without boiling, until the sugar has dissolved. Increase the heat and bring to the boil. Brush down the side of the pan with a pastry brush dipped in water to prevent sugar crystals from forming. Reduce the heat and simmer, without stirring, until the mixture turns dark brown and begins to smell burnt.

2 Put a tea towel in the sink to stand the pan on (the sink may buckle if it is not protected). Transfer the pan to the sink, place a tea towel over your arm to protect it and add 185 ml (6 fl oz/¾ cup) of water to the pan. The mixture will splutter violently. When the spluttering subsides, return the pan to medium heat and stir with a wooden spoon until the caramel dissolves and comes to the boil. Reduce the heat and simmer for 1 minute.

3 Set aside in the pan to cool, then pour into an airtight container and refrigerate overnight for the sauce to thicken.

 Serve with waffles and ice cream, pancakes or crepes. Also good with fresh or poached fruit.

Butterscotch Sauce

Serves 6

125 g (4^1/$_2$ oz) butter
90 g (3^1/$_4$ oz/^{1}/$_2$ cup) soft brown sugar
2 tablespoons golden syrup (see note)
125 ml (4 fl oz/^{1}/$_2$ cup) cream (whipping)
1 teaspoon natural vanilla extract

1   Put the butter and brown sugar in a saucepan and stir over low heat until the butter has melted and the sugar has dissolved.

2   Bring to the boil and add the golden syrup and cream. Reduce the heat and simmer for 10 minutes, or until the sauce has thickened slightly. Remove from the heat and add the vanilla. Serve hot or cold.

Note: If preferred, reduce the butter to 60 g (2^1/$_4$ oz) and omit the golden syrup.

 Serve with grilled (broiled) bananas, peaches or nectarines, fresh fruit, steamed puddings, waffles or crepes.

Caramel Rum Sauce

Serves 6

225 g (8 oz/1 cup) caster (superfine) sugar
200 ml (7 fl oz) thick (double/heavy) cream
50 g (1³/4 oz) butter
2 tablespoons dark rum

1 Put the sugar and 150 ml (5 fl oz) of water in a saucepan and stir until the sugar has dissolved. Bring to the boil and continue to boil until golden brown.

2 Remove from the heat and add the cream. Re-dissolve any lumps, then add the butter and rum. Stir until smooth. Serve warm.

 Serve on steamed puddings or ice cream.

Caramel Sauce

Serves 6

225 g (8 oz/1 cup) caster (superfine) sugar
400 g (14 oz) condensed milk
1 tablespoon golden syrup, optional
1 teaspoon natural vanilla extract

1. Put the sugar and 60 ml (2 fl oz/¼ cup) of water in a small heavy-based saucepan. Stir over low heat, without boiling, for 10 minutes, or until the sugar has dissolved. Brush any crystals from the side of the pan with a wet pastry brush.

2. Increase the heat to medium and simmer, without stirring, until the mixture turns a deep caramel colour. Remove from the heat and, using a tea towel to protect your hands, slowly and carefully pour on 125 ml (4 fl oz/½ cup) of hot water. The caramel will spit when the hot water is added, so take care.

3. Return the saucepan to low heat and stir until the caramel has melted again. Remove from the heat and stir in the condensed milk, golden syrup, if using, and vanilla. Serve warm or chilled. The sauce will thicken when refrigerated.

 Serve with ice cream, pancakes, steamed puddings or cakes.

Cherry Sauce

Serves 4

3 x 425 g (15 oz) tins pitted black cherries
115 g (4 oz/$\frac{1}{2}$ cup) caster (superfine) sugar
1 vanilla bean, split lengthways
1 cinnamon stick
2 star anise

1   Drain the cherries, reserving 170 ml (5$\frac{1}{2}$ fl oz/$\frac{2}{3}$ cup) of the syrup. Put the cherries, syrup, sugar, vanilla bean, cinnamon stick and star anise in a saucepan.

2   Simmer, stirring occasionally, for 25 minutes, or until the sugar has dissolved and the sauce is thick and syrupy. Remove the vanilla bean, cinnamon stick and star anise. Serve warm or cold.

 Serve with waffles and ice cream or chocolate cake.

Chocolate Cherry Sauce

Serves 6

425 g (15 oz) tin pitted black cherries
100 ml (3¹/₂ fl oz) cream (whipping)
200 g (7 oz/1¹/₃ cups) chopped dark chocolate

1 Drain the cherries, reserving 2 tablespoons of the syrup.

2 Put the cream and chocolate in a heatproof bowl. Bring a
   saucepan of water to the boil, then remove from the heat.
   Sit the bowl over the pan, making sure the base of the
   bowl does not touch the water. Stir occasionally until the
   chocolate has melted and combined with the cream.

3 Stir the cherries and reserved syrup into the chocolate
   mixture. Serve warm.

 Serve with pancakes and ice cream.

Chocolate Fudge Sauce

Serves 8

250 g (9 oz/1²/3 cups) chopped good-quality
  dark chocolate
185 ml (6 fl oz/³/4 cup) cream (whipping)
50 g (1³/4 oz) butter
1 tablespoon golden syrup or corn syrup
2 tablespoons Baileys, Tia Maria or Kahlúa

1 Place the chocolate, cream, butter and golden syrup or corn
  syrup in a saucepan. Stir over low heat until the chocolate
  has melted and the mixture is smooth.

2 Stir in the liqueur. Serve hot or cold.

 Serve with ice cream, profiteroles,
waffles, pancakes, poached fruit or
steamed puddings.

Chocolate Orange Sauce

Serves 8

3 large strips orange zest, white pith removed
125 ml (4 fl oz/$1/2$ cup) orange juice
2 tablespoons caster (superfine) sugar
200 g (7 oz/$11/3$ cups) chopped milk chocolate
300 ml ($101/2$ fl oz) cream (whipping)
2 teaspoons Cointreau or other orange liqueur

1 Put the orange zest and orange juice in a small saucepan and bring to the boil. Stir in the sugar, then simmer for 3 minutes, or until the mixture is thick and syrupy and reduced to 2 tablespoons. Set aside to cool, then cut the zest into thin strips.

2 Put the chocolate in a heatproof bowl. Bring the cream to the boil, then pour it over the chocolate and set aside for 2 minutes. Stir until the chocolate has melted, then stir in the orange syrup, orange zest and liqueur. Serve warm.

 Serve over profiteroles or ice cream.

Chocolate Rum Sauce

serves 8

185 g (6¹/2 oz/1 cup) soft brown sugar
60 g (2¹/4 oz) butter
185 ml (6 fl oz/³/4 cup) cream (whipping)
1 tablespoon dark rum
60 g (2¹/4 oz/¹/2 cup) chopped dark chocolate

1 Put the sugar, butter and cream in a saucepan. Bring to the boil, stirring, over gentle heat. Reduce the heat and simmer for 4 minutes.

2 Remove from the heat and add the rum and chocolate. Stir until the chocolate has melted. Cool to room temperature before serving, to allow the sauce to thicken slightly.

 Serve with pancakes, waffles, steamed puddings, brownies, ice cream or fruit kebabs.

Chocolate Sauce

Serves 4

40 g (1^1/$_2$ oz) butter
30 g (1 oz/^{1}/$_4$ cup) cocoa powder, sifted
185 g (6^1/$_2$ oz/1 cup) soft brown sugar
300 ml (10^1/$_2$ fl oz) cream (whipping)

1 Put the butter, cocoa and brown sugar in a saucepan and mix well.

2 Add the cream and stir over low heat until the sauce comes to the boil. Serve hot.

 Serve over ice cream, profiteroles, waffles or pancakes.

Citrus Syrup

Serves 8

350 g (12 oz/1½ cups) caster (superfine) sugar
3 strips citrus zest, white pith removed
80 ml (2½ fl oz/⅓ cup) lemon, lime, orange or mandarin juice

1 Put the sugar, zest, juice and 80 ml (2½ fl oz/⅓ cup) of water in a saucepan. Stir over low heat, without boiling, until the sugar has dissolved.

2 Bring to the boil, then reduce the heat and simmer for 12–15 minutes, or until the syrup has slightly thickened. Remove the zest before serving. Serve warm or cold.

 Serve over a hot or cold cake.

Coconut Lime Anglaise

Serves 4

3 egg yolks
55 g (2 oz/¼ cup) caster (superfine) sugar
1 teaspoon cornflour (cornstarch)
185 ml (6 fl oz/¾ cup) coconut cream
125 ml (4 fl oz/½ cup) milk
60 ml (2 fl oz/¼ cup) cream (whipping)
1 teaspoon finely grated lime zest

1 Whisk the egg yolks, sugar and cornflour in a heatproof bowl with electric beaters until light and creamy.

2 Put the coconut cream, milk, cream and lime zest in a small saucepan and heat until almost boiling, then pour onto the egg mixture, beating constantly.

3 Return the mixture to the saucepan and stir over low heat for about 5 minutes, or until slightly thickened — do not allow the sauce to boil or it will curdle.

4 Strain the sauce into a chilled heatproof bowl and serve immediately, or cover the surface with plastic wrap to prevent a skin forming and serve cold.

Serve with steamed puddings, poached fruit or jelly desserts.

Coffee Anglaise

Serves 4-6

2 egg yolks
2 tablespoons caster (superfine) sugar
250 ml (9 fl oz/1 cup) milk
1¹/2 teaspoons instant coffee granules

1 Beat the egg yolks and sugar in a mixing bowl until light and creamy.

2 Put the milk and coffee granules in a saucepan and stir over medium heat until the coffee has dissolved. Bring to the boil, then remove from the heat and gradually whisk in the egg yolk mixture.

3 Stir constantly over low heat for 5 minutes, or until the mixture coats the back of a spoon — do not allow the sauce to boil or it will curdle.

4 Remove the pan from the heat and transfer the sauce to a bowl. Serve immediately, or cover the surface with plastic wrap to prevent a skin forming and serve cold.

 Serve over steamed puddings, dessert muffins or mousse.

Coffee Cream Sauce

Serves 8–10

55 g (2 oz/¼ cup) caster (superfine) sugar
90 g (3¼ oz/½ cup) soft brown sugar
250 ml (9 fl oz/1 cup) cream (whipping)
1½ tablespoons instant coffee powder
2 tablespoons Tia Maria or other coffee liqueur, optional

1 Put the caster sugar, brown sugar, cream and coffee powder in a small saucepan. Stir over medium heat, without boiling, until the sugars have completely dissolved.

2 Bring to the boil, then reduce the heat and simmer for 3 minutes, or until the mixture has thickened slightly. Stir in the liqueur, if using. Serve warm.

 Serve over steamed puddings.

Crème Anglaise

Serves 4

3 egg yolks
2 tablespoons caster (superfine) sugar
375 ml (13 fl oz/1½ cups) milk
½ teaspoon natural vanilla extract

1 Whisk the egg yolks and sugar in a heatproof bowl for 2 minutes, or until light and creamy. Heat the milk in a small saucepan until almost boiling, then pour onto the egg mixture, whisking constantly.

2 Return the mixture to the pan and stir over low heat for about 5 minutes, or until slightly thickened, enough to coat the back of a spoon. Do not allow the custard to boil or it will curdle.

3 Remove the pan from the heat and stir in the vanilla. Transfer the sauce to a bowl and serve immediately, or cover the surface with plastic wrap to prevent a skin forming and serve cold.

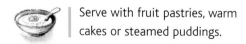 Serve with fruit pastries, warm cakes or steamed puddings.

Hard Sauce

Serves 8

125 g (4¹/2 oz) unsalted butter
250 g (9 oz/2 cups) sifted icing (confectioners') sugar
1 tablespoon brandy, whisky or rum

1 Beat the butter in a bowl until soft. Gradually add the icing sugar and beat until the mixture is light and creamy.

2 Beat in the brandy, whisky or rum. Cover and refrigerate until firm.

 Serve with plum pudding.

Jam Sauce

Serves 8

310 g (11 oz/1 cup) jam
1 teaspoon finely grated lemon zest
caster (superfine) sugar, to taste

1 Combine the jam, lemon zest and 250 ml (9 fl oz/1 cup) of water in a small saucepan. Stir over medium heat, then reduce the heat slightly and bring to the boil.

2 Reduce the heat and simmer for 10 minutes. Stir in the sugar, to taste. Serve warm.

 Serve with ice cream and warm cakes or steamed puddings.

Lemon and Lime Sauce

Serves 4–6

225 g (8 oz/1 cup) caster (superfine) sugar
60 ml (2 fl oz/¼ cup) lemon juice
60 ml (2 fl oz/¼ cup) lime juice
2 tablespoons vodka
1 tablespoon chopped mint
zest of 1 lemon, white pith removed, cut into fine strips

1 Put the sugar, lemon juice, lime juice and 250 ml (9 fl oz/ 1 cup) of water in a saucepan. Stir over low heat until the sugar has dissolved. Slowly bring to the boil, then reduce the heat and simmer, without stirring, until the mixture has thickened to a syrupy consistency.

2 Remove the pan from the heat, stir in the vodka and set aside to cool.

3 Add the mint and strips of lemon zest and pour into a sterilized jar. Store the sauce in the refrigerator for up to two weeks.

Serve over fresh fruit such as sliced oranges, or use as a poaching liquid for fruit.

Mango Coulis

Serves 6

2 mangoes, peeled and seeded
2–4 tablespoons icing (confectioners') sugar, or to taste
1 tablespoon lemon juice
1–2 tablespoons Cointreau or other orange liqueur

1 Purée the mango flesh in a food processor.

2 Add the sugar and lemon juice and process until smooth. Stir in the liqueur.

 Serve with fresh or poached fruit, soufflés, ice cream, sorbet, pies or tarts.

Maple Sauce

Serves 4–6

90 ml (3 fl oz) cream (whipping)
2 tablespons pure maple syrup
25 g (1 oz) unsalted butter
pinch of freshly grated nutmeg

1 Put the cream, maple syrup, butter and nutmeg in a saucepan. Stir over low heat until the butter has melted, then simmer for 5 minutes, or until thickened slightly. Set aside to cool until just warm.

 Serve with steamed puddings or warm cakes.

Marsala Sauce

Serves 4

125 ml (4 fl oz/^{1}/2 cup) sweet Marsala
80 g (2^3/4 oz/^{1}/3 cup) caster (superfine) sugar

1 Combine the Marsala and sugar in a small saucepan. Stir over low heat until the sugar has dissolved.

2 Heat until just boiling, then reduce the heat and simmer for 4–5 minutes, or until just syrupy — do not overcook or the sauce will harden when cool. Remove from the heat and serve warm.

 Serve with vanilla ice cream.

Mocha Sauce

Serves 8

60 g (2¹/₄ oz) butter
150 g (5¹/₂ oz/1 cup) chopped dark chocolate
375 ml (13 fl oz/1¹/₂ cups) cream (whipping)
1 tablespoon instant coffee powder
2 tablespoons crème de cacao or other
   chocolate liqueur, optional

1 Combine the butter, chocolate, cream and coffee powder in a saucepan. Stir over low heat until the butter and chocolate have melted and the mixture is smooth.

2 Remove from the heat and stir in the liqueur, if using. Serve warm.

 Serve with vanilla or chocolate steamed pudding or ice cream.

Mousseline

Serves 4

90 g (3¹/₄ oz) butter
1 tablespoon lemon juice
2 egg yolks
1 teaspoon sugar
grated zest of 1 orange
60 ml (2 fl oz/¹/₄ cup) cream (whipping), whipped

1 Melt the butter and lemon juice in a small saucepan, then bring to the boil.

2 Put the egg yolks in a blender. With the motor running, add the butter and lemon mixture; the mixture will thicken as the hot liquid cooks the yolks.

3 Stir in the sugar and grated orange zest, then fold in the whipped cream.

 Serve with fresh or grilled (broiled) fruit such as figs.

Muscat Cream

Serves 8-10

300 g (10^1/$_2$ oz/1^1/$_4$ cups) sour cream
50 g (1^3/$_4$ oz/^{1}/$_4$ cup) soft brown sugar
1 egg yolk
2 tablespoons liqueur muscat or sweet sherry

1 Beat the sour cream, brown sugar and egg yolk with electric beaters for 5 minutes, or until thick and glossy.

2 Beat in the liqueur muscat or sherry. Cover and refrigerate for at least 2 hours before serving.

 Serve in place of whipped cream with warm pastries, fruit tarts, steamed puddings or fresh fruit.

Orange Cream Sauce

Serves 6–8

300 ml (10½ fl oz) cream (whipping)
2 tablespoons orange juice
1 tablespoon grated orange zest
1 teaspoon natural vanilla extract

1 Combine the cream, orange juice, orange zest and vanilla in a bowl and mix well.

 Serve with steamed puddings.

Orange Liqueur Sauce

Serves 4

1/2 teaspoon grated orange zest

185 ml (6 fl oz/3/4 cup) orange juice

2 tablespoons caster (superfine) sugar

2 tablespoons Cointreau or other orange liqueur

1 tablespoon cornflour (cornstarch)

30 g (1 oz) butter, cubed

1 Put the orange zest, orange juice, sugar and liqueur in a small saucepan.

2 Blend the cornflour with 60 ml (2 fl oz/1/4 cup) of water until smooth. Add to the saucepan and stir over low heat for 3–4 minutes, or until the mixture boils and thickens. Add the butter and stir for 1 minute. Serve warm.

 Serve with crepes or pancakes.

Orange Sauce

Serves 4

120 g (4¼ oz) butter, cubed
115 g (4 oz/½ cup) caster (superfine) sugar
1 teaspoon grated orange zest
80 ml (2½ fl oz/⅓ cup) orange juice

1   Melt the butter in a small saucepan over medium heat. Add the sugar and stir until dissolved.

2   Add the orange zest and orange juice and mix well. Bring to the boil, then reduce the heat and simmer for 1–2 minutes, or until the sauce is slightly reduced and syrupy. Serve warm.

 Serve with pancakes and ice cream.

Passionfruit Sauce

Serves 8

185 g (6^1/$_2$ oz/^{3}/$_4$ cup) passionfruit pulp (6–8 passionfruit)
60 ml (2 fl oz/^{1}/$_4$ cup) orange juice
2 tablespoons caster (superfine) sugar
1 tablespoon cornflour (cornstarch)

1 Strain the passionfruit to separate the juice and seeds — you will need 125 ml (4 fl oz/^{1}/$_2$ cup) of passionfruit juice and 1^1/$_2$ tablespoons of seeds. Put the passionfruit juice, seeds, orange juice and sugar in a small saucepan.

2 Mix the cornflour with 60 ml (2 fl oz/^{1}/$_4$ cup) of water until smooth, then add to the passionfruit mixture. Stir over medium heat until the mixture boils and thickens. Serve warm or cold.

 Serve with steamed puddings, pancakes or waffles.

Pecan Butterscotch Sauce

Serves 4

20 g (³/4 oz) butter
115 g (4 oz/²/3 cup) soft brown sugar
125 ml (4 fl oz/¹/2 cup) cream (whipping)
2 tablespoons chopped pecans

1 Put the butter, brown sugar and cream in a saucepan. Stir over low heat for 4 minutes, or until the sugar has dissolved and the butter has melted.

2 Stir in the chopped pecans. Serve warm.

 Serve with pancakes or waffles and ice cream.

Praline Cream Sauce

Serves 6

80 g (2³/4 oz/¹/2 cup) roasted blanched almonds
115 g (4 oz/¹/2 cup) caster (superfine) sugar
100 g (3¹/2 oz/¹/3 cup) chocolate hazelnut spread
300 ml (10¹/2 fl oz) cream (whipping)

1   Arrange the almonds in a single layer on a lined baking tray.

2   Combine the sugar with 80 ml (2¹/2 fl oz/¹/3 cup) of water
in a small saucepan. Stir over low heat, without boiling,
until the sugar has dissolved. Cook, without stirring, until
the mixture turns golden, then quickly pour it over the
almonds. Allow to set until hard, then process the praline
in a food processor until it is broken into fine crumbs.

3   Put the hazelnut spread in a heatproof bowl over a
saucepan of hot water until the spread softens slightly.
Remove the bowl from the pan and stir in the cream. Whisk
until smooth (do not overbeat or the sauce will become
grainy), then fold in the praline crumbs and serve.

 Serve with fresh or poached
fruit, pancakes, crepes or
chocolate cake.

Raisin Butterscotch Sauce

Serves 6

2 tablespoons brandy
40 g (1 1/2 oz/1/3 cup) raisins
80 ml (2 1/2 fl oz/1/3 cup) cream (whipping)
60 g (2 1/4 oz) butter, cubed
50 g (1 3/4 oz/1/4 cup) soft brown sugar

1 Put the brandy and raisins in a small saucepan and stir over medium heat for 5 minutes. Transfer to a bowl.

2 Put the cream, butter and brown sugar in the same saucepan and stir until the sugar begins to dissolve and the butter begins to melt. Bring to the boil, then reduce the heat and simmer for 5 minutes, or until the mixture thickens slightly. Pour into the bowl with the brandied raisins and mix well. Serve warm.

 Serve with ice cream.

Raspberry Coulis

Serves 8

300 g (10^1/$_2$ oz/2^1/$_2$ cups) raspberries
30 g (1 oz/^{1}/$_4$ cup) icing (confectioners') sugar
1 teaspoon lemon juice

1   Process the raspberries and sugar in a food processor for
    20 seconds, or until smooth. Add the lemon juice, to taste.

 Serve with ice cream, sorbet
or cheesecake.

Raspberry Sauce

Serves 6

225 g (8 oz/1 cup) caster (superfine) sugar
1 cinnamon stick
125 g (4¹/₂ oz/1 cup) raspberries
125 ml (4 fl oz/¹/₂ cup) good-quality red wine

1 Put the sugar and 250 ml (9 fl oz/1 cup) of water in a saucepan. Stir over medium heat, without boiling, until the sugar has completely dissolved.

2 Add the cinnamon stick and simmer for 5 minutes. Add the raspberries and wine and boil rapidly for 5 minutes.

3 Discard the cinnamon stick and push the sauce through a sieve, discarding the seeds. Cool and then chill the sauce before serving.

 Serve with panna cotta or chocolate mousse.

Rhubarb Sauce

Serves 6

350 g (12 oz) rhubarb, chopped
90 g (3¼ oz/½ cup) soft brown sugar
¼ teaspoon mixed (pumpkin pie) spice

1 Put the rhubarb, sugar, mixed spice and 250 ml (9 fl oz/ 1 cup) of water in a saucepan. Bring to the boil, stirring to dissolve the sugar. Reduce the heat and simmer, stirring often, for 10 minutes.

2 Set aside to cool slightly, then purée the sauce in a blender or food processor until smooth. Serve hot or cold.

 Serve with cheesecakes or ice cream.

Sherry Mousseline

Serves 6–8

1 egg
1 egg yolk
2 tablespoons caster (superfine) sugar
2 tablespoons sherry

1 Combine the egg, egg yolk, sugar and sherry in a heatproof bowl and place over a saucepan of just simmering water.

2 Beat with electric beaters for 5–8 minutes, or until the mixture is thick and frothy. Serve immediately.

 Serve with steamed puddings.

Strawberry Sauce

Serves 6-8

55 g (2 oz/¼ cup) caster (superfine) sugar
250 g (9 oz/1²/³ cups) strawberries
2 tablespoons brandy or strawberry liqueur

1 Put the sugar and 60 ml (2 fl oz/¼ cup) of water in a saucepan and heat until the sugar has dissolved. Add the strawberries and simmer for 5 minutes. Remove from the heat and set aside to cool slightly.

2 Process the strawberry mixture in a food processor for 30 seconds, or until smooth. Stir in the brandy or strawberry liqueur, to taste. Serve warm or cold.

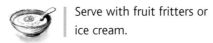 Serve with fruit fritters or ice cream.

Vanilla Cream Sauce

Serves 6

250 ml (9 fl oz/1 cup) cream (whipping)
125 ml (4 fl oz/1/2 cup) milk
3 egg yolks
1 teaspoon cornflour (cornstarch)
2 tablespoons caster (superfine) sugar
1/2 teaspoon natural vanilla extract

1 Heat the cream and milk together in a saucepan until almost boiling.

2 Beat the egg yolks, cornflour and sugar in a small bowl with electric beaters. Pour the hot cream mixture over the yolks, beating continuously.

3 Return the mixture to the saucepan and stir over low heat, without boiling, until the sauce is smooth. Strain the sauce into a cold bowl. Stir in the vanilla and chill before serving.

 Serve with poached fruit.

Vanilla Custard

Serves 6

250 ml (9 fl oz/1 cup) milk
60 ml (2 fl oz/¼ cup) cream (whipping)
3 egg yolks
80 g (2¾ oz/⅓ cup) caster (superfine) sugar
2 teaspoons cornflour (cornstarch)
1 teaspoon natural vanilla extract

1 Put the milk and cream in a saucepan and bring to the boil. Immediately remove the pan from the heat.

2 Whisk the egg yolks, sugar and cornflour in a heatproof bowl. Slowly pour the hot milk mixture over the egg mixture, whisking continuously.

3 Return the mixture to the saucepan and stir over low heat, without boiling, for 5 minutes, or until the custard starts to bubble and thicken. Remove from the heat immediately. Whisk in the vanilla and serve warm.

Serve with sweet pies, pastries or steamed puddings.

Whisky Sauce

Serves 8–10

50 g (1³/₄ oz) butter
40 g (1¹/₂ oz/¹/₃ cup) plain (all-purpose) flour
500 ml (17 fl oz/2 cups) milk
2 tablespoons caster (superfine) sugar
80 ml (2¹/₂ fl oz/¹/₃ cup) whisky
1 tablespoon thick (double/heavy) cream

1 Melt 40 g (1¹/₂ oz) of the butter in a saucepan over low heat. Remove from the heat, add the flour and stir until combined. Gradually whisk in the milk and sugar.

2 Stir over medium heat until the sauce boils and thickens. Reduce the heat and simmer, stirring occasionally, for 10 minutes.

3 Remove from the heat and stir in the whisky, cream and remaining butter. Cover the surface with plastic wrap to prevent a skin forming until ready to serve.

 Serve with plum pudding.

White Chocolate Sauce

Serves 8

125 g (4½ oz/1 cup) chopped good-quality white chocolate
80 ml (2½ fl oz/⅓ cup) cream (whipping)

1 Put the white chocolate and cream in a small heatproof bowl and place over a small saucepan of simmering water, making sure the base of the bowl doesn't touch the water.

2 Stir until the sauce is melted and smooth, then set aside to cool slightly before serving.

 Serve with cheesecake or berries.

Zabaglione

Serves 10-12

8 egg yolks
80 g (2³/4 oz/¹/3 cup) caster (superfine) sugar
310 ml (10³/4 fl oz/1¹/4 cups) sweet Marsala

1 Beat the egg yolks and sugar in a heatproof bowl with electric beaters until pale yellow.

2 Put the bowl over a gently simmering pan of water and beat continuously, adding the Marsala gradually. Beat for 5 minutes, or until thick and frothy. To test if it is ready, dip a metal spoon into the sauce and hold it up — if the mixture slides down the back it is not yet thickened enough. If you can draw a line through the sauce with a spoon and leave a trail, it is ready. Serve immediately or serve chilled.

 Serve with savoiardi (lady fingers), fresh berries, poached or grilled (broiled) fruits.

index